KATE HALE

Managing Burnout and Fatigue

Recognizing Early Signs and Taking Action

Copyright © 2024 by KATE HALE

All rights reserved. No part of this publication may be reproduced, stored or transmitted in any form or by any means, electronic, mechanical, photocopying, recording, scanning, or otherwise without written permission from the publisher. It is illegal to copy this book, post it to a website, or distribute it by any other means without permission.

First edition

This book was professionally typeset on Reedsy. Find out more at reedsy.com

Contents

Introduction	1
What Is Burnout?	6
Early Signs and Symptoms	10
Understanding Fatigue	15
Work-Related Burnout	23
Personal Factors Contributing to Burnout	28
Lifestyle Triggers and Modern Pressures	34
Building Self-Awareness	41
Lifestyle Adjustments to Combat Burnout	46
Setting Boundaries and Prioritizing Self-Care	53
Building Resilience in High-Stress Jobs	61
Communicating Effectively with Employers	68
Creating a Supportive Work Environment	76
Rediscovering Passion and Purpose	83
Maintaining Long-Term Balance	89
Conclusion	96

Introduction

Understanding Burnout and Fatigue

Burnout and fatigue are two critical issues in today's fast-paced society, especially with the increasing demands placed on individuals in both personal and professional spheres. Burnout, a term widely discussed in occupational psychology, is characterized by a state of emotional, physical, and mental exhaustion caused by excessive and prolonged stress. This condition is commonly linked to workplace stressors; however, it can emerge from other parts of life as well, such as managing personal responsibilities, relationship challenges, or simply enduring ongoing pressure without sufficient rest or recovery. Fatigue, while often associated with burnout, differs in that it's typically characterized by a pervasive sense of tiredness or lack of energy that can affect both body and mind. Unlike burnout, which is often situational and related to external pressures, fatigue can arise from various factors, including health issues, inadequate sleep, and lifestyle choices.

The impact of burnout and fatigue on individuals cannot be overstated. Both can lead to diminished productivity, strained relationships, and, in severe cases, lasting health concerns. Chronic fatigue can cause a host of physical health issues, including a weakened immune system, high blood pressure, and even an increased risk of chronic conditions such as heart disease and diabetes. Burnout, on the other hand, tends to have a more pronounced effect on mental health, leading to symptoms like depression, anxiety, irritability, and a sense of hopelessness or disillusionment. Recognizing and understanding these conditions are essential steps toward managing them effectively and restoring a sense of balance and well-being.

Despite their prevalence, burnout and fatigue are often misunderstood or dismissed, either due to misconceptions around their causes and symptoms or because of societal pressures that discourage individuals from acknowledging these states of exhaustion. Many people believe that pushing through is a sign of strength and resilience, but ignoring these signs only leads to further harm over time. Understanding the nuances between burnout and fatigue can empower individuals to address these conditions in their early stages and prevent them from spiraling into more severe problems.

Why Recognizing Early Signs Matters

Recognizing the early signs of burnout and fatigue is crucial, as early intervention can help prevent these conditions from escalating. When left unchecked, burnout and fatigue can become chronic, leading to a cycle of exhaustion and disengagement that can be hard to break. Early signs of burnout may include subtle behavioral changes, such as losing interest in work or hobbies, withdrawing from social interactions, and experiencing feelings of irritability or frustration over minor inconveniences. Fatigue, on the other hand, often starts with physical symptoms like difficulty waking up in the morning, a persistent feeling of tiredness, and reduced physical endurance.

By learning to recognize these initial signs, individuals can take proactive steps to adjust their routines, seek support, and make necessary lifestyle changes before these conditions worsen. Recognizing burnout early, for example, might involve identifying when stressors are becoming overwhelming and implementing stress-management techniques such as mindfulness or physical activity to reduce their impact. Similarly, identifying early signs of fatigue can encourage individuals to assess factors like their sleep patterns, diet, and exercise routines, which often play a significant role in energy levels.

In workplaces, recognizing early signs is equally important. Managers and employers can benefit from understanding how to identify burnout in their teams, as it helps them create a supportive environment that prioritizes well-being. For instance, if a manager notices an employee consistently struggling with workload, they might offer adjustments or additional resources to alleviate the pressure. Additionally, prioritizing mental health and wellness in the workplace can lead to increased productivity, reduced absenteeism, and overall higher job satisfaction among employees. In personal contexts, recognizing these signs allows friends and family members to offer support, whether it's by providing a listening ear, assisting with daily tasks, or encouraging the affected person to seek professional help.

Early recognition also plays a crucial role in breaking the stigma associated with burnout and fatigue. Many individuals hesitate to acknowledge their struggles, fearing that it will make them appear weak or incapable. When people understand that these conditions are common and manageable, they are more likely to seek help. Openly addressing burnout and fatigue can foster a culture where individuals feel supported and empowered to take action, benefiting both their personal and professional lives.

Myths and Misconceptions About Burnout

A common misconception about burnout is that it only affects those in high-stress jobs. While individuals in demanding professions—such as healthcare, law, and education—are indeed at a higher risk, burnout can impact anyone. Stay-at-home parents, students, and even retirees can experience burnout if they are dealing with continuous stressors and lack adequate coping mechanisms. Burnout is not limited to professional stress; it can also be a result of emotional and personal pressures that accumulate over time, making it essential for everyone to remain vigilant about their mental and physical well-being.

Another myth surrounding burnout is the notion that it's simply a result of poor time management or lack of personal resilience. This misunderstanding places undue blame on the individual, overlooking the broader systemic factors that often contribute to burnout. While effective time management and personal resilience can help mitigate stress, burnout is frequently influenced by factors outside an individual's control, such as workplace culture, societal pressures, and unrealistic expectations. For example, an employee may face burnout due to an unmanageable workload or lack of support from their organization, situations that cannot be solved through time management alone.

Many people also believe that burnout is simply a passing phase or that it can be resolved with a short break or vacation. While taking time off can provide temporary relief, burnout often requires deeper, long-term changes to fully recover. Returning to the same environment without addressing the root causes of burnout can quickly lead to a recurrence of symptoms. Sustainable recovery from burnout involves assessing and adjusting various aspects of one's life, including workload, work-life balance, and self-care practices. This may include setting boundaries, seeking professional help, or finding new ways to recharge regularly.

There is also a misconception that burnout is a sign of failure or inadequacy. This belief can make individuals reluctant to admit they are experiencing burnout, as they may fear judgment or repercussions. However, burnout is a widespread and well-documented phenomenon that many people face at some point in their lives. Recognizing burnout as a legitimate issue that anyone can experience helps stigmatize it, making it easier for individuals to seek help without feeling ashamed.

A significant myth surrounding fatigue is that it is merely a result of inadequate sleep. While sleep is undeniably essential, fatigue can stem from a variety of factors, including emotional stress, poor diet, lack of physical activity, and underlying medical conditions. Addressing fatigue often requires

INTRODUCTION

a multifaceted approach that goes beyond simply increasing the number of hours spent in bed. People who view fatigue solely as a sleep-related issue may neglect other critical areas of their lifestyle that could be contributing to their exhaustion.

Lastly, many believe that burnout and fatigue are solely individual problems that should be managed privately. In reality, these issues often have societal and cultural dimensions. For example, a work culture that rewards over-working and penalizes resting can contribute significantly to burnout among employees. Similarly, societal expectations around constant productivity and achievement can lead to chronic fatigue in individuals who feel compelled to keep up. Recognizing burnout and fatigue as collective issues that require systemic change allows for a broader, more supportive approach to addressing them.

What Is Burnout?

Burnout is a state of physical, emotional, and mental exhaustion that typically results from prolonged stress, often due to relentless work pressures or personal responsibilities. While burnout is closely associated with professional environments, it can arise in any situation where individuals are subject to ongoing stress, such as care giving, studying, or even managing household responsibilities. Burnout manifests as a pervasive sense of fatigue, detachment, and decreased effectiveness, impacting an individual's overall well-being and quality of life.

Burnout and fatigue are often discussed together, but they are distinct phenomena. Fatigue is primarily characterized by physical tiredness and reduced energy levels. It can be caused by a lack of sleep, overexertion, or even poor diet and is typically alleviated through rest and recovery. Burnout, however, is a more complex condition that encompasses emotional and mental exhaustion. While physical fatigue can contribute to burnout, the latter involves an additional layer of emotional strain that impacts motivation, self-perception, and one's ability to cope with stress. Burnout is not something that can be remedied simply by taking a few days off; it requires a deeper, more sustained approach to recovery.

The concept of burnout is often broken down into three primary dimensions: emotional exhaustion, depersonalize, and reduced personal accomplishment. Emotional exhaustion refers to the feeling of being completely drained and unable to muster the energy to continue with day-to-day responsibilities.

Individuals experiencing emotional exhaustion often feel overwhelmed and may begin to dread tasks that once felt manageable or even enjoyable. This dimension is commonly the first sign of burnout, manifesting as feelings of fatigue, irritability, and a sense of dread surrounding daily responsibilities.

Depersonalize, the second dimension, is characterized by a sense of detachment or estrangement from one's work or responsibilities. Individuals experiencing depersonalize may become cynical or develop negative attitudes toward their tasks, coworkers, or even the clients or individuals they serve. This detachment often serves as a coping mechanism, as individuals attempt to shield themselves from the emotional toll of their responsibilities. However, this sense of detachment can also lead to a lack of empathy and reduced interpersonal engagement, affecting both personal and professional relationships.

The third dimension, reduced personal accomplishment, involves a decline in self-efficacy and satisfaction in one's abilities. Individuals in this phase of burnout may begin to doubt their skills, feel ineffective, or lose confidence in their ability to achieve meaningful results. This loss of self-assurance often compounds the feelings of emotional exhaustion and depersonalize, creating a cycle of self-doubt and decreased motivation. As a result, the person experiencing burnout may withdraw from tasks and responsibilities, which can lead to further frustration and feelings of failure.

The triggers and causes of burnout are varied and can include both external and internal factors. Common triggers include high workloads, tight deadlines, and lack of autonomy. In workplace settings, burnout often arises when individuals feel they lack control over their tasks or responsibilities, leading to a sense of helplessness. Long hours and a lack of work-life balance further exacerbate this issue, as individuals have little opportunity to recharge or engage in activities that provide relief from stress.

Interpersonal conflicts are another significant cause of burnout. Tensions with colleagues, supervisors, or clients can create a toxic work environment, heightening stress and making it difficult for individuals to feel supported or valued. When employees feel isolated or misunderstood, their emotional resilience is often compromised, making them more susceptible to burnout. This isolation can also contribute to the sense of depersonalize, as individuals may start to distance themselves emotionally to protect against the impact of negative interactions.

In many cases, burnout is also rooted in personal expectations and perfectionist tendencies. Individuals who set high standards for themselves, or who are highly invested in their roles, may experience burnout when they feel they are not meeting their goals or when their contributions go unrecognized. Perfectionism often drives individuals to work harder and longer, leading to exhaustion and, ultimately, a sense of failure when they are unable to achieve their self-imposed standards. This internalized pressure can be particularly detrimental, as it often makes individuals reluctant to seek help or admit they are struggling.

Moreover, burnout can be exacerbated by broader societal and cultural pressures. In many cultures, there is an emphasis on productivity and success, with individuals often equating their self-worth with their accomplishments. This societal value system places pressure on individuals to constantly push themselves, often at the expense of their health and well-being. In environments where overwork is glorified, individuals may feel guilty for taking time to rest, which only compounds the problem and can accelerate the onset of burnout.

Finally, technological advancements and the modern work environment contribute significantly to burnout. With the rise of remote work, the boundaries between personal and professional life have become increasingly blurred, making it difficult for individuals to disconnect. The constant connectivity facilitated by digital devices means that many individuals are expected to be available around the clock, responding to emails, messages, and work-related notifications even outside of regular hours. This constant connectivity prevents individuals from fully disengaging from their work, leading to chronic stress and, over time, burnout.

In essence, burnout is a complex condition rooted in both personal and environmental factors. It affects individuals in all walks of life, from corporate executives to caregivers and students. Recognizing the symptoms and understanding the dimensions of burnout—emotional exhaustion, depersonalize, and reduced personal accomplishment—are essential steps in addressing the issue and preventing its recurrence.

Early Signs and Symptoms

The early signs and symptoms of burnout are often subtle and can be easily mistaken for normal stress, tiredness, or lack of motivation. However, recognizing these early indicators is critical to preventing the condition from escalating into severe burnout, which can have significant impacts on both mental and physical health. Burnout manifests through a range of physical, emotional, and behavioral symptoms that, when recognized early, provide an opportunity to take action before reaching a critical level of exhaustion and detachment.

The physical signs of burnout are often the most noticeable but are also frequently ignored or attributed to other causes. Persistent fatigue, for example, is one of the earliest physical signs of burnout. This goes beyond simple tiredness; it's a type of exhaustion that doesn't improve with a night's rest or even a weekend off. Individuals may feel a lingering lack of energy, experiencing difficulties waking up in the morning and a sense of dread for the day ahead. This persistent fatigue can progress to physical ailments, such as headaches, muscle tension, and back pain, which are all stress-related but may become chronic if burnout is left unaddressed. Digestive issues are also common, as stress impacts the body's digestive processes, leading to symptoms like nausea, stomach cramps, or changes in appetite.

Beyond fatigue, individuals experiencing burnout may also notice a general decline in their immune system. When under prolonged stress, the body's immune response weakens, making one more susceptible to infections and illnesses. This often leads to a cycle where individuals experience frequent colds or illnesses, which only further drain their already depleted energy levels. Moreover, sleep disturbances are prevalent, with individuals experiencing either insomnia—difficulty falling or staying asleep—or hypermedia, where they sleep excessively but still wake up feeling untested.

Emotional signs of burnout are equally telling but can be more challenging to recognize as they often blend with other aspects of daily life. Increased irritability and feelings of frustration are common early signs. Individuals might find themselves losing their temper over minor inconveniences or feeling disproportionately annoyed by situations that wouldn't usually bother them. This irritation is often accompanied by a sense of emotional numbness or detachment. Many people begin to feel apathetic or indifferent toward their work, responsibilities, or even relationships, viewing them as obligations rather than meaningful aspects of their lives. This emotional disconnection can lead to feelings of isolation, as individuals may withdraw from social interactions, feeling that others can't understand what they're going through.

Burnout also manifests in negative self-perception and self-doubt. Those experiencing burnout often struggle with feelings of inadequacy, believing they are not performing well or not living up to their potential. This self-criticism can turn into a pervasive sense of guilt, especially for those who are accustomed to high levels of productivity. They may feel guilty for not meeting their usual standards, which only adds to their stress and exacerbates their emotional exhaustion. These feelings can further spiral into more intense emotions such as anxiety or depression, with individuals experiencing constant worry, sadness, or hopelessness about their situation.

The behavioral signs of burnout are often where the condition becomes more noticeable to others. Individuals may begin to disengage from their usual activities and responsibilities, showing a decline in productivity or a lack of motivation. They might start procrastinating, taking longer to complete tasks, or finding themselves distracted more easily. This lack of focus and motivation can lead to a reduced quality of work and an overall sense of dissatisfaction, both for the individual and those around them, such as colleagues or family members. Moreover, individuals experiencing burnout may engage in avoidance behaviors, such as calling in sick more frequently, leaving work early, or avoiding responsibilities altogether.

Another significant behavioral indicator is increased reliance on unhealthy coping mechanisms. To manage stress and emotional exhaustion, individuals may turn to habits such as excessive caffeine or alcohol consumption, overeating, or even drug use. These coping strategies provide temporary relief but often worsen the overall condition, as they can lead to further health complications or deepen feelings of guilt and self-blame. Over time, these behaviors can become destructive, further impacting an individual's physical and mental health.

Differentiating between stress and burnout is essential because, while they share some similarities, they require different approaches for effective management. Stress is often short-term and can be managed with techniques such as relaxation exercises, time management, and physical activity. It is usually characterized by over-engagement; stressed individuals tend to feel hyperactive, anxious, and often respond with urgency. Burnout, on the other hand, is a state of disengagement and emotional numbness. It occurs when stress becomes chronic and is no longer effectively managed, leading to an exhaustion that cannot be easily remedied.

One way to distinguish between stress and burnout is by observing one's emotional response to challenges. In stressful situations, individuals are usually highly reactive and feel overwhelmed by demands. However, they may still feel a sense of urgency to complete their tasks and achieve their goals. In burnout, this emotional response shifts to indifference or apathy. Challenges no longer evoke a strong reaction; instead, individuals feel detached and unmotivated, viewing tasks as burdens rather than goals to accomplish. Additionally, stress often leaves individuals feeling exhausted at the end of the day but able to recharge with rest, while burnout's exhaustion is more profound and persists despite efforts to rest.

Burnout also has a more severe impact on one's mental health. Prolonged stress can lead to anxiety, but burnout frequently results in feelings of hopelessness, despair, and depression. Individuals may experience a sense of disillusionment, feeling as though their efforts are meaningless. This lack of purpose and motivation is a hallmark of burnout and sets it apart from regular stress, which typically doesn't affect one's sense of personal accomplishment or purpose as drastically.

To recognize and address burnout effectively, self-assessment tools can be invaluable. Self-assessment questionnaires, like the Maslach Burnout Inventory (MBI) or the Copenhagen Burnout Inventory (CBI), provide structured ways for individuals to evaluate the intensity of their symptoms and the degree of their burnout. These tools often assess key aspects such as emotional exhaustion, depersonalize, and reduced personal accomplishment, helping individuals gauge whether they are experiencing burnout or simply high levels of stress. While these assessments are not diagnostic tools, they offer insight into areas that may require attention and intervention.

Another practical self-assessment tool is journalism, which allows individuals to track their energy levels, mood, and emotional responses over time. By recording daily thoughts and feelings, individuals can identify patterns that may indicate early signs of burnout. For example, if someone consistently notes feelings of fatigue, irritability, or disengagement, these recurring observations can serve as a red flag. Journalism also allows individuals to reflect on specific stressors, helping them understand what aspects of their lives are contributing most to their burnout and what changes might be necessary.

Mindfulness practices are also beneficial for recognizing burnout. Regular mindfulness exercises encourage individuals to focus on the present moment, allowing them to become more aware of their mental and physical states. Through mindfulness, individuals can better recognize when they are feeling exhausted, anxious, or disconnected, as these practices help develop an awareness of one's internal state. This awareness can serve as an early warning system, alerting individuals to potential burnout before it becomes severe.

Finally, talking openly with trusted friends, family members, or even a mental health professional can provide invaluable insights. Others may observe changes in behavior or mood that an individual might not recognize, and their feedback can be instrumental in helping someone understand whether they are exhibiting signs of burnout. Supportive conversations can also offer relief and validation, as discussing one's experiences with someone who listens and understands can alleviate some of the emotional burden associated with burnout.

By identifying physical, emotional, and behavioral signs, distinguishing between stress and burnout, and utilizing self-assessment tools, individuals can gain a clearer understanding of their mental and physical health. Early intervention is critical, as recognizing these signs early on can help prevent burnout from escalating, allowing individuals to seek support and make necessary lifestyle adjustments before their health and well-being are severely impacted.

Understanding Fatigue

Fatigue is a pervasive and complex phenomenon that affects nearly everyone at some point in life. It can be described as a persistent feeling of tiredness, lack of energy, or weariness that affects one's ability to perform daily tasks effectively. Unlike simple tiredness that can be relieved with rest, fatigue often lingers and can significantly impact physical, mental, and emotional health. Understanding the different types of fatigue—physical, mental, and emotional—as well as recognizing the distinctions between chronic fatigue syndrome and temporary fatigue, is essential in identifying the underlying causes and finding effective ways to manage it. Fatigue manifests in various ways in daily life, often affecting multiple areas and impeding one's ability to function optimally.

The first type of fatigue, physical fatigue, is often the most recognizable and is primarily characterized by a sense of physical exhaustion or a lack of energy in the body. Physical fatigue typically stems from prolonged physical exertion, insufficient rest, or health conditions that impair physical function. It might be experienced as muscle weakness, reduced endurance, or an inability to perform physical activities that were once manageable. For example, an individual experiencing physical fatigue might struggle with everyday tasks such as climbing stairs, carrying groceries, or engaging in exercise. This form of fatigue is also commonly seen in individuals who lead sedentary lifestyles, as a lack of regular physical activity can lead to a decline in physical stamina and overall energy levels. While physical fatigue can often be alleviated through rest, hydration, and balanced nutrition, chronic physical fatigue may signal underlying medical conditions, such as anemia, hypothyroidism, or cardiovascular issues.

Physical fatigue can also arise from conditions that disrupt the body's normal functioning, such as sleep disorders like insomnia, sleep apnea, or restless legs syndrome. When the body doesn't receive adequate rest, it cannot restore energy levels effectively, leading to a constant feeling of tiredness regardless of how much sleep one gets. Physical fatigue is often accompanied by other symptoms, such as headaches, dizziness, and muscle aches, which further impact one's ability to function. Moreover, chronic illnesses, such as autoimmune disorders and diabetes, can contribute to physical fatigue, as the body is constantly fighting inflammation, regulating blood sugar levels, or managing other physiological imbalances that drain energy resources. For those affected by chronic physical fatigue, managing symptoms requires more than rest; it involves medical intervention, lifestyle changes, and potentially, long-term management strategies to improve overall quality of life.

Mental fatigue is another type of fatigue that significantly impacts cognitive function and productivity. Unlike physical fatigue, which primarily affects the body, mental fatigue is a state of mental exhaustion where the brain becomes overwhelmed or overstimulated, resulting in reduced concentration, difficulty making decisions, and a decline in memory and focus. Mental fatigue often occurs in individuals who face high cognitive demands, such as students, professionals, and caregivers who must remain attentive and responsive over extended periods. For instance, someone who spends hours solving complex problems, managing numerous responsibilities, or constantly switching between tasks may experience mental fatigue. This type of fatigue is exacerbated by the modern digital lifestyle, where individuals are bombarded with information and frequently multitask, making it challenging for the brain to fully recharge.

The symptoms of mental fatigue often include a sense of "brain fog," where individuals feel mentally sluggish, forgetful, or struggle to focus on tasks. Decision-making becomes more challenging, as mental fatigue impairs cognitive flexibility, making it harder to evaluate options, process information, and select appropriate responses. Additionally, mental fatigue can result in irritability and frustration, as individuals become less tolerant of interruptions or complex tasks. When left unaddressed, mental fatigue can lead to burnout, as the brain remains in a constant state of overdrive without the necessary rest and recovery. Strategies to manage mental fatigue often involve regular breaks, setting boundaries to limit information overload, and engaging in activities that promote relaxation and cognitive refreshment, such as meditation, deep breathing exercises, or engaging in a hobby that doesn't require intense focus.

Emotional fatigue is a third type of fatigue that affects one's emotional resilience and overall mood. Emotional fatigue often results from prolonged exposure to stressful situations or environments that demand a high degree of emotional investment. Individuals experiencing emotional fatigue might feel emotionally drained, apathetic, or disconnected from their surroundings. This form of fatigue is common among caregivers, healthcare workers, and individuals in high-stress environments, where they are required to be emotionally present, supportive, or compassionate, often at the expense of their own well-being. Over time, this constant emotional exertion depletes one's emotional reserves, making it difficult to cope with even minor stressors.

The symptoms of emotional fatigue are often subtle but can have profound effects on an individual's quality of life. Individuals may become more sensitive to criticism, feel overwhelmed by minor challenges, or experience a sense of detachment from their work or relationships. This emotional numbness often leads to disengagement, where individuals lose interest in activities or relationships that once brought them joy. Emotional fatigue can also manifest as irritability or heightened emotional responses, where individuals become easily frustrated, sad, or even angry without clear reasons. These symptoms can impact relationships, as emotional fatigue often leads to misunderstandings and conflicts with loved ones or colleagues. To manage emotional fatigue, individuals may need to seek support, whether through talking to friends and family, engaging in therapy, or practicing self-care routines that allow them to replenish their emotional energy.

In some cases, fatigue becomes more than a temporary experience and develops into a condition known as chronic fatigue syndrome (CFS). Chronic fatigue syndrome, also known as myalgic encephalomyelitis (ME), is a complex disorder characterized by severe, persistent fatigue that does not improve with rest and is often worsened by physical or mental activity. Unlike temporary fatigue, which usually has a clear cause and can be alleviated through rest or lifestyle changes, CFS presents as a long-term health condition that significantly impacts an individual's quality of life. Symptoms of CFS include refreshing sleep, memory problems, muscle and joint pain, headaches, and a heightened sensitivity to physical exertion, known as post-exertional malaise. Individuals with CFS often find that even small tasks can trigger debilitating fatigue that lasts for days or weeks.

The exact cause of CFS remains unclear, but research suggests it may be linked to immune system abnormalities, hormonal imbalances, or viral infections. The onset of CFS often occurs after an illness, such as the flu or mononucleosis, but it can also emerge following periods of significant stress. Diagnosing CFS can be challenging, as there are no specific tests for the condition, and its symptoms overlap with other illnesses. Therefore, CFS is often diagnosed by ruling out other possible causes of chronic fatigue. Individuals with CFS may require a multidisciplinary approach to treatment, including medication, physical therapy, and lifestyle adjustments, as well as psychological support to cope with the emotional impact of living with a chronic condition.

Temporary fatigue, on the other hand, is a short-term experience that is usually tied to identifiable causes, such as insufficient sleep, intense physical activity, or brief periods of stress. Unlike CFS, temporary fatigue can often be resolved with rest, hydration, or changes to one's daily routine. For example, a person who feels fatigued after a long day at work may recover with a good night's sleep or a day off. Temporary fatigue is a natural response to physical or mental exertion and is not typically cause for concern unless it becomes persistent. However, recurring temporary fatigue could indicate underlying issues, such as poor sleep hygiene, an imbalanced diet, or unaddressed stress, and may eventually lead to more chronic forms of fatigue if not managed effectively.

Fatigue manifests in various ways in daily life, affecting everything from work performance to personal relationships. Physically, fatigue often reduces one's motivation to engage in exercise or physical activity, leading to a sedentary lifestyle. This lack of physical activity can further exacerbate fatigue, as regular exercise is essential for maintaining energy levels and overall health. Individuals experiencing fatigue may also find it challenging to maintain a consistent routine, as the effort required to complete tasks becomes increasingly burdensome. For instance, someone who experiences persistent fatigue might struggle to keep up with household chores, meal preparation, or personal care, as these tasks feel overwhelming and exhausting.

In the workplace, fatigue can result in reduced productivity, as individuals find it difficult to concentrate, remember information, or stay engaged with their tasks. Fatigue often leads to an increase in mistakes or missed deadlines, as the brain struggles to process information and maintain focus. Additionally, fatigue can hinder creativity and problem-solving abilities, as mental resources are drained, leaving little energy for innovative thinking or complex tasks. Over time, this decline in work performance can lead to feelings of frustration, self-doubt, and even job dissatisfaction, as individuals may feel they are no longer able to meet their own standards or the expectations of their employers.

In personal relationships, fatigue can strain communication and emotional connection. Individuals experiencing emotional or mental fatigue may have little energy left for social interactions, leading them to withdraw from family and friends. This withdrawal can create feelings of loneliness or isolation, as individuals feel misunderstood or unsupported in their struggles. Emotional fatigue, in particular, can make it challenging to empathize with others or engage in meaningful conversations, as individuals are emotionally drained and have little capacity for additional emotional engagement. This can lead to conflicts, as loved ones may misinterpret fatigue-related withdrawal as disinterest or lack of care.

Fatigue also impacts one's ability to engage in leisure activities and hobbies. For many, hobbies provide a source of joy, relaxation, and personal fulfillment. However, when fatigue sets in, even enjoyable activities can feel like chores. Individuals may lose interest in their hobbies, as the effort required to engage feels overwhelming. This can lead to a cycle where the individual becomes further disconnected from sources of joy and relaxation, exacerbating feelings of fatigue and disconnection from life.

Ultimately, fatigue affects nearly every aspect of daily life, creating a ripple effect that impacts physical health, mental clarity, emotional stability, and social connections. Over time, unaddressed fatigue can lead to more severe consequences, including mental health issues such as depression or anxiety. Persistent fatigue may also influence lifestyle choices, as individuals might turn to stimulants like caffeine or energy drinks to maintain alertness or, conversely, to substances like alcohol to manage the emotional strain, creating a cycle that only deepens fatigue in the long run.

Addressing fatigue effectively requires a multifaceted approach that considers its various sources and manifestations. For physical fatigue, prioritizing sleep hygiene, balanced nutrition, and regular exercise is fundamental. Sleep hygiene involves maintaining a consistent sleep schedule, creating a restful sleeping environment, and avoiding stimulating activities before bed to ensure restorative sleep. Physical activity, though it may seem counter intuitive for someone who is tired, has been shown to increase energy levels and improve overall stamina by enhancing circulation and oxygen flow throughout the body.

Mental fatigue, on the other hand, benefits from techniques that allow the brain to rest and recharge. Practices such as mindfulness, taking regular breaks, and scheduling "digital detox" periods where one disconnects from electronic devices can help reduce mental overload. Engaging in leisure activities that don't demand intense cognitive effort, such as listening to music, reading a novel, or spending time in nature, can also provide mental relief.

Emotional fatigue requires emotional support and healthy coping mechanisms. Developing a strong support network of friends, family, or professional counselors can provide the emotional outlet needed to process difficult experiences and feelings. Practices like journalism can help individuals identify and articulate sources of emotional stress, enabling them to manage these feelings in a structured way. Additionally, setting healthy boundaries to limit exposure to emotionally draining situations or individuals can preserve emotional resources, allowing individuals to focus on their own well-being.

Recognizing the distinction between temporary fatigue and chronic fatigue conditions, such as chronic fatigue syndrome (CFS), is crucial. While temporary fatigue can typically be managed with lifestyle adjustments and self-care practices, chronic fatigue may require a more comprehensive treatment plan. Individuals with CFS often benefit from a multidisciplinary approach that includes physical therapy, dietary modifications, medication, and psychological support to address the broad range of symptoms. Since CFS remains a poorly understood condition, ongoing research and patient education are essential to providing effective support and improving quality of life for those affected.

In sum, fatigue is a multidimensional issue that affects individuals on physical, mental, and emotional levels, influencing nearly every aspect of daily life. By understanding the different types of fatigue, recognizing the early signs, and employing targeted strategies for management, individuals can take proactive steps to mitigate its impact. Whether caused by physical strain, mental overload, or emotional stress, addressing fatigue holistically empowers individuals to lead more balanced and fulfilling lives, fostering resilience and improved well-being in the face of life's many demands.

Work-Related Burnout

Complex and widespread issue that affects individuals across various industries and job roles, and it has only intensified with modern work demands. Burnout is not simply the result of working long hours; it is often rooted in a combination of factors that create an environment where people feel overwhelmed, unsupported, and, ultimately, disconnected from their work. Understanding the root causes of work-related burnout, such as workload and work-life imbalance, toxic work environments, poor leadership, job insecurity, and the fear of failure, is essential in addressing and preventing this pervasive issue.

A significant contributor to work-related burnout is workload and work-life imbalance. The demands of modern workplaces frequently exceed what many employees can sustainably manage, leading to a chronic state of exhaustion and stress. This imbalance often results from excessive workloads, tight deadlines, and expectations for productivity that require constant effort. In some industries, working long hours is seen as a badge of honor, creating a culture where employees feel pressured to sacrifice personal time and rest to meet work demands. This expectation erodes the boundary between work and personal life, making it difficult for individuals to recharge and maintain their well-being.

In many cases, technological advancements have intensified workload pressures. Remote work and digital connectivity blur the line between working hours and personal time, as employees often feel obligated to respond to emails, messages, or tasks outside of traditional hours. This constant availability can be exhausting, as individuals struggle to mentally detach from work. Over time, this lack of separation between work and personal life leads to physical and emotional exhaustion, reducing job satisfaction and increasing the likelihood of burnout.

Furthermore, the inability to achieve a healthy work-life balance can lead to guilt and frustration, especially for those who value personal responsibilities, such as family commitments or self-care. When work demands infringe upon these areas, individuals often feel as though they are failing in multiple domains of their lives, which compounds the stress. This emotional toll can erode personal relationships and reduce engagement with hobbies or activities that bring joy and relaxation, further contributing to the sense of burnout. To combat this, organizations and individuals must prioritize boundaries, recognizing that sustainable productivity requires time for rest, recreation, and self-care.

Another critical factor in work-related burnout is toxic work environments and poor leadership. Toxic workplaces are characterized by a lack of respect, fairness, and support, as well as by high levels of conflict, micromanagement, or favoritism. In such environments, employees often feel undervalued, misunderstood, and even threatened. These negative experiences lead to feelings of alienation, distrust, and chronic stress, all of which contribute to burnout. Toxic work environments can arise in any industry, and they are often exacerbated by leadership that either directly contributes to or fails to address these issues.

Poor leadership plays a significant role in shaping the workplace culture and employee experiences. Leaders who engage in unfair practices, such as favoritism or arbitrary decision-making, create an environment where employees feel unsupported and unappreciated. Similarly, micromanagement—where leaders closely control every aspect of an employee's work—erodes autonomy and trust, making employees feel powerless. Without the ability to exercise independence, employees often lose motivation and engagement, as they feel their contributions are neither valued nor trusted. This lack of control is a powerful contributor to burnout, as individuals become disillusioned with their role and may feel trapped in an oppressive work environment.

On the other hand, a lack of guidance and support from leadership can be equally detrimental. When employees do not receive adequate feedback, direction, or resources, they may feel lost and uncertain about their responsibilities or performance. This ambiguity creates a state of chronic stress, as individuals worry about meeting expectations without clear parameters for success. In such situations, employees are more likely to internalize failures or missteps, believing that they are personally responsible for not meeting expectations. Over time, this sense of inadequacy erodes confidence and increases the emotional toll of work, contributing to burnout.

Workplace bullying or harassment is another aspect of toxic work environments that has a profound impact on mental health and well-being. When individuals experience bullying from colleagues or supervisors, it creates an atmosphere of fear and humiliation. This constant exposure to negative treatment not only affects job satisfaction but also leads to feelings of worthlessness, isolation, and severe stress. In extreme cases, victims of workplace bullying may develop symptoms of depression, anxiety, or post-traumatic stress disorder (PTSD). Organizations have a responsibility to foster a supportive and respectful work environment, as failure to address toxic behaviors can have long-term effects on employee health, morale, and productivity.

Job insecurity and the fear of failure are also prominent contributors to work-related burnout. In today's competitive and often unpredictable job market, many individuals face constant anxiety about job stability. Economic factors, organizational restructuring, or the prevalence of temporary contracts create a pervasive sense of insecurity, as employees worry that their positions may be at risk. This lack of stability places employees in a heightened state of alertness, as they constantly feel the need to prove their worth to avoid potential layoffs. Over time, this anxiety takes a toll, leading to stress and burnout as individuals operate under the constant pressure to perform and secure their role.

The fear of failure is closely intertwined with job insecurity, as individuals feel that even minor mistakes or setbacks could jeopardize their employment. In high-stakes environments, where performance is closely monitored and success is defined by strict metrics, individuals may experience paralyzing self-doubt and anxiety. This fear of failure often leads to perfectionism, where individuals go to extreme lengths to avoid errors, working long hours and scrutinizing their work in minute detail. While striving for excellence can be beneficial, perfectionism rooted in fear is counterproductive, as it drains mental and emotional resources. Over time, this hyper-focus on avoiding failure can create a vicious cycle, where individuals become so consumed by anxiety that they are unable to function effectively, further perpetuating the risk of burnout.

Job insecurity also has an impact on workplace relationships, as individuals may feel reluctant to seek support or collaborate openly with colleagues out of fear that showing vulnerability could be seen as a weakness. This isolation exacerbates feelings of stress, as employees lack the emotional support and camaraderie that help mitigate work-related challenges. In contrast, employees who feel secure in their roles are more likely to form positive relationships, collaborate effectively, and seek assistance when needed. Job security provides a foundation of stability, allowing individuals to focus on their work without the constant fear of losing their livelihood.

In some cases, the fear of failure is also driven by self-imposed expectations, where individuals hold themselves to exceptionally high standards. This type of internalized pressure can be equally damaging, as individuals are constantly battling their own perceived shortcomings. When they inevitably encounter setbacks, they may interpret these as evidence of their inadequacy, which fuels further anxiety and self-doubt. Without a balanced perspective on success and failure, individuals risk becoming trapped in a cycle of self-criticism, making it difficult to feel a sense of accomplishment or satisfaction in their work. Over time, this internal pressure erodes confidence and resilience, making individuals more susceptible to burnout.

In summary, work-related burnout is often rooted in a combination of factors, each of which contributes to a work environment where individuals feel overwhelmed, unsupported, and anxious about their roles. The pressure of high workloads and the challenge of achieving work-life balance create an ongoing state of physical and mental exhaustion. Toxic work environments and poor leadership amplify these stresses by eroding trust, autonomy, and support. Job insecurity and the fear of failure further compound the issue, as individuals struggle with self-doubt and worry about the stability of their employment. Addressing these root causes requires a concerted effort from both organizations and individuals to foster a work culture that prioritizes well-being, respect, and a sense of security. By recognizing and addressing these factors, workplaces can reduce the risk of burnout and create a healthier, more productive environment for all employees.

Personal Factors Contributing to Burnout

Burnout is often influenced by external factors such as workplace demands or environmental stressors. However, it's essential to recognize that personal traits and lifestyle choices can significantly contribute to burnout, making individuals more vulnerable to its effects. Characteristics like perfectionism, tendencies toward over achievement, lack of boundaries, people-pleasing behaviors, and ongoing financial or relationship stress can all serve as catalysts for burnout. These internal factors often intertwine with external pressures, creating a complex web of stress that can be difficult to manage. Understanding these personal factors is crucial for recognizing how individuals may inadvertently increase their own risk of burnout and for developing strategies to address these challenges.

One of the most prominent personal factors contributing to burnout is perfectionism and over achievement. Perfectionists often set unrealistically high standards for themselves, believing that anything less than flawless performance is unacceptable. This mindset creates a constant pressure to perform at peak levels, leading individuals to invest excessive time and effort into tasks to ensure they meet their own rigorous expectations. While striving for excellence can be a positive trait, perfectionism rooted in fear of failure or a need for approval is detrimental. It fuels a relentless cycle of self-criticism and dissatisfaction, as perfectionists are rarely satisfied with their accomplishments, no matter how objectively successful they may be.

Perfectionists may also struggle to delegate tasks, believing that others cannot meet the same high standards. This often results in them taking on more work than they can manage, which only compounds their stress and exhaustion. The inability to delegate stems from a lack of trust in others' abilities, as well as the belief that their reputation or self-worth is tied to their output. As a result, perfectionists often feel overburdened, which leads to a gradual depletion of their physical, mental, and emotional resources. This prolonged state of stress and exhaustion is a significant contributor to burnout, as individuals become trapped in an unsustainable cycle of overwork and self-criticism.

Over achievement is closely related to perfectionism but carries a distinct set of characteristics. Overachievers are driven by a desire to accomplish as much as possible, often at the expense of their own well-being. While they may not always hold themselves to impossibly high standards, they tend to overload their schedules with tasks, projects, and goals in an effort to maximize productivity and success. Overachievers are often motivated by external rewards such as recognition, promotions, or financial incentives, which reinforces their drive to constantly push their limits. However, this focus on achievement often leads to a neglect of self-care and personal needs, as overachievers prioritize work over rest, relaxation, and personal fulfillment.

The tendency toward over achievement can create a pattern of chronic stress and exhaustion, as individuals feel compelled to maintain high levels of productivity regardless of their own capacity. This unyielding drive to achieve leaves little room for recovery, increasing the risk of burnout over time. Overachievers may also struggle with feelings of inadequacy or imposer syndrome, as they constantly compare themselves to others and worry that they are not doing enough. This fear of inadequacy can lead to anxiety, self-doubt, and a sense of being perpetually "behind," further exacerbating the emotional strain that contributes to burnout.

Another key personal factor that contributes to burnout is a lack of boundaries and a tendency toward people-pleasing. Individuals who lack boundaries often find it difficult to say no, taking on more responsibilities and commitments than they can realistically manage. People-pleasers, in particular, are driven by a desire to gain approval, avoid conflict, or make others happy, often at the expense of their own needs. They may feel guilty or anxious about setting limits, fearing that they will disappoint others or be perceived as uncooperative. This reluctance to establish boundaries creates a situation where individuals feel overwhelmed, as they are constantly accommodating others' requests and expectations.

The lack of boundaries can lead to burnout by leaving individuals with little time or energy for themselves. When individuals are constantly giving to others—whether at work, in personal relationships, or within their communities—they deplete their own emotional resources. Without adequate time for rest, self-care, or personal fulfillment, they become more vulnerable to exhaustion and resentment. This dynamic is particularly challenging for those in care giving roles, such as healthcare workers, teachers, or parents, as these roles often involve high levels of emotional labor. The constant need to be available for others creates a sense of obligation and guilt, making it difficult for individuals to prioritize their own well-being.

People-pleasers may also experience burnout due to the emotional toll of constantly seeking approval and validation. This external focus means that people-pleasers are often hyper-aware of others' opinions and reactions, which can lead to heightened stress and anxiety. When they feel that they have failed to meet someone ease's expectations, they may experience self-blame and shame, further compounding their emotional exhaustion. Over time, this pattern of people-pleasing leads to a loss of self-identity, as individuals become so focused on meeting others' needs that they lose sight of their own values, goals, and desires. This disconnect from one's own needs and priorities is a significant factor in burnout, as individuals feel unfulfilled and disconnected from their own lives.

Financial and relationship stress are additional personal factors that can contribute to burnout, as they create a pervasive sense of insecurity and worry that affects nearly every aspect of life. Financial stress, in particular, is a significant source of anxiety for many individuals, as it impacts their ability to meet basic needs, achieve personal goals, and feel secure in their future. The pressure to manage debt, save for major expenses, or simply cover daily living costs can create a constant state of worry and tension. Financial stress often leads to overwork, as individuals take on additional jobs or work longer hours to make ends meet. This constant effort to achieve financial stability can lead to physical and mental exhaustion, as individuals push themselves to their limits in pursuit of security.

In addition to the physical demands of overwork, financial stress can lead to feelings of inadequacy or shame, particularly in a society that places a high value on financial success. Individuals who struggle financially may feel as though they have failed or that they are not living up to societal expectations, which can lead to a loss of self-worth. This emotional toll further exacerbates stress, creating a vicious cycle where individuals feel trapped by their circumstances. The combination of physical exhaustion from overwork and emotional strain from financial insecurity is a powerful contributor to burnout, as individuals feel unable to escape the pressures they face.

Relationship stress is another factor that can significantly impact mental and emotional well-being, increasing the risk of burnout. Relationships—whether romantic, familial, or social—are a fundamental part of life and provide essential support and connection. However, when relationships are strained or dysfunctional, they can become a source of stress rather than relief. Conflict, lack of communication, and emotional distance can all create a sense of isolation and anxiety, leaving individuals feeling unsupported in their challenges. In some cases, individuals may feel obligated to maintain relationships that are draining or even toxic, which can take a heavy toll on their mental health.

For individuals experiencing relationship stress, the emotional energy required to navigate conflict or maintain a strained connection can lead to feelings of exhaustion and depletion. This emotional labor is particularly taxing when individuals feel responsible for the well-being of others, as is often the case in care giving roles or relationships where there is a significant power imbalance. Over time, this constant emotional effort erodes resilience, leaving individuals vulnerable to burnout. Relationship stress can also exacerbate feelings of self-doubt, as individuals may question their own worth or feel as though they are failing to meet others' expectations.

In cases where both financial and relationship stress are present, the risk of burnout is even greater, as individuals feel overwhelmed by the demands of managing multiple sources of stress simultaneously. The combination of financial insecurity and strained relationships creates a pervasive sense of instability, as individuals lack both the material resources and emotional support needed to cope with challenges. This state of chronic stress can lead to a sense of hopelessness, as individuals feel trapped in their circumstances with no clear path to relief.

To address the personal factors contributing to burnout, individuals must first recognize and acknowledge these influences in their lives. Perfectionists and overachievers, for example, can benefit from challenging their own beliefs about success and self-worth, learning to set realistic expectations and to celebrate progress rather than perfection. Practicing self-compassion and developing a growth mindset can help individuals reduce self-criticism and develop a healthier relationship with achievement. For those struggling with a lack of boundaries or people-pleasing tendencies, learning to set limits and prioritize personal needs is essential. This may involve practicing assertive communication, recognizing that saying no is not a failure, and seeking validation from within rather than relying on others' approval.

Addressing financial and relationship stress often requires a combination of practical and emotional strategies. Financial counseling or budgeting resources can help individuals create a sense of control over their finances, while support from mental health professionals or support groups can provide relief from the emotional strain of financial stress. In relationships, open communication and boundary-setting are essential for reducing stress and fostering healthy connections. For those in toxic or harmful relationships, seeking support to establish safety and self-care is crucial for preventing burnout and promoting well-being.

By understanding the personal factors contributing to burnout—such as perfectionism, lack of boundaries, and financial or relationship stress—individuals can develop targeted strategies for managing these influences and fostering resilience. Recognizing these internal challenges allows individuals to make conscious choices that prioritize well-being, create balance, and build a more fulfilling, sustainable life free from the cycle of burnout.

Lifestyle Triggers and Modern Pressures

In our fast-paced, digitally connected world, modern pressures and lifestyle choices play a significant role in contributing to burnout and overall well-being. While burnout was once considered primarily work-related, it's increasingly clear that lifestyle choices and societal influences also shape how individuals experience stress and exhaustion. Factors such as digital overload, lack of sleep, poor nutrition, and societal expectations collectively impact our mental and physical health, fueling a cycle of fatigue and stress. By examining these lifestyle triggers, we can gain insight into how to better manage our environments and daily habits, fostering resilience and a balanced approach to modern life.

The impact of digital overload and social media on mental health and burnout cannot be overstated. Digital devices and social media platforms have become deeply integrated into daily life, shaping how we interact with the world, how we work, and how we view ourselves. While these tools offer convenience and connectivity, they also demand our constant attention, contributing to cognitive overload and emotional strain. The omnipresence of technology has made it challenging to disconnect, with people spending hours scrolling through social media feeds, reading news updates, or checking work emails. This continuous exposure to information, coupled with the pressure to be constantly available, has created an environment where individuals struggle to mentally "switch off."

Digital overload manifests in several ways, including decreased attention span, difficulty focusing, and a constant need for stimulation. With each notification, message, or social media post, individuals experience a brief spike in dopamine—a neurotransmitter associated with pleasure and reward. Over time, however, this constant stimulation conditions the brain to crave more frequent bursts of information, making it difficult to engage in sustained focus on tasks that require deep concentration. As a result, many individuals find it increasingly challenging to complete tasks, read long texts, or engage in face-to-face conversations without feeling the urge to check their devices. This fragmented attention can lead to feelings of frustration, irritability, and fatigue, as individuals struggle to maintain focus in both work and personal settings.

Social media, in particular, has its own unique impact on mental health and burnout. While social media allows individuals to connect with others and share experiences, it also exposes them to constant comparisons and unrealistic standards. Platforms like Instagram, Facebook, and Twitter often present an idealized version of life, where people showcase their accomplishments, appearance, and lifestyle. This curated reality can lead to feelings of inadequacy and self-doubt, as individuals compare their own lives to the seemingly perfect lives they see online. This phenomenon, known as "social comparison," has been linked to increased rates of anxiety, depression, and low self-esteem, as individuals feel that they are falling short of societal standards. Furthermore, the pressure to present a curated online identity can create a sense of disconnection, as individuals prioritize appearances over authenticity, leading to emotional exhaustion.

The continuous influx of news and information on digital platforms can also contribute to emotional burnout, especially in an era where global events, crises, and controversies are constantly broadcaster. The phenomenon of "doom scrolling," where individuals compulsively consume negative news, has been linked to heightened anxiety and feelings of hopelessness. As people absorb distressing information about the world, they may feel overwhelmed, helpless, and emotionally drained. This exposure to distressing news can activate the brain's stress response, making it difficult to disengage from feelings of anxiety and worry. Over time, this cycle of digital consumption and emotional burnout takes a toll on mental health, leading to fatigue, decreased productivity, and a diminished sense of well-being.

Lack of sleep and poor nutrition are other significant lifestyle factors that contribute to burnout and overall health. Sleep is essential for physical and mental restoration, allowing the body to repair itself, process emotions, and consolidate memories. However, modern lifestyles often prioritize productivity over rest, leading to a culture where sleep is sacrificed in favor of work, social activities, or digital engagement. Chronic sleep deprivation has been linked to a host of health issues, including weakened immune function, impaired cognitive performance, and increased risk of mental health disorders. Individuals who consistently fail to get adequate sleep often experience symptoms of fatigue, irritability, and difficulty concentrating, all of which are common precursors to burnout.

One of the reasons sleep is often sacrificed is the constant presence of digital devices, which emit blue light that disrupts the body's natural sleep-wake cycle, or circadian rhythm. Blue light exposure in the evening suppresses the production of melatonin, a hormone that signals to the body that it's time to sleep. As a result, individuals who use electronic devices before bed often struggle to fall asleep or experience poor-quality sleep. This cycle of disrupted sleep can lead to a cumulative sleep deficit, where the body is never fully rested, leaving individuals feeling exhausted and more susceptible to stress. Over time, chronic sleep deprivation can also impair decision-making, memory, and emotional regulation, making it difficult to cope with daily challenges and increasing vulnerability to burnout.

Poor nutrition further exacerbates the effects of sleep deprivation and contributes to burnout by depriving the body of essential nutrients needed for energy, focus, and resilience. The modern diet, often high in processed foods, refined sugars, and unhealthy fats, lacks the nutritional value required to support optimal brain and body function. Nutrient deficiencies, particularly in vitamins B, D, and magnesium, have been linked to fatigue, mood disturbances, and impaired cognitive function. When individuals rely on convenience foods or skip meals due to busy schedules, they deprive their bodies of the fuel needed to function effectively, leading to physical and mental exhaustion.

Dietary habits, such as excessive caffeine or sugar intake, can also have a counterproductive effect on energy levels. While caffeine provides a temporary energy boost, excessive consumption can lead to jitteriness, anxiety, and sleep disruptions, ultimately exacerbating fatigue. Similarly, foods high in sugar cause blood sugar spikes, followed by crashes, which can leave individuals feeling sluggish and irritable. This roller coaster effect on energy levels creates a cycle where individuals rely on stimulants to get through the day, only to experience a deeper crash later, perpetuating feelings of exhaustion and burnout. A balanced diet rich in whole foods, lean proteins, healthy fats, and complex carbohydrates is essential for sustaining energy levels, stabilizing mood, and promoting resilience against stress.

The influence of societal expectations also plays a significant role in shaping modern stress levels and contributing to burnout. Society often promotes ideals of success, productivity, and self-sufficiency, placing immense pressure on individuals to achieve and excel in multiple areas of life. These expectations are particularly evident in the workplace, where employees are often encouraged to work long hours, pursue continuous self-improvement, and achieve tangible markers of success, such as promotions, awards, or salary increases. While ambition and hard work are valuable traits, the societal expectation to constantly strive for success can create a relentless cycle of pressure, leading individuals to overextend themselves without regard for their well-being.

In addition to career-related pressures, societal expectations around personal appearance, lifestyle, and social status contribute to burnout by creating a sense of inadequacy and self-criticism. The media often portrays images of physical beauty, luxury lifestyles, and success that are difficult, if not impossible, to attain. These representations fuel a culture of comparison, where individuals feel pressured to conform to unrealistic standards. This desire to meet societal expectations can lead to unhealthy behaviors, such as overworking, dieting, or engaging in excessive exercise, as individuals attempt to attain the idealized versions of success and beauty promoted by society. The constant effort to meet these standards, combined with the fear of judgment or failure, creates a state of chronic stress that erodes self-esteem and contributes to burnout.

Societal expectations around gender roles and care giving responsibilities also influence burnout, particularly for individuals who face added pressure to fulfill roles as both professionals and caregivers. Women, for example, often experience the "second shift," where they manage professional responsibilities during the day and take on care giving or household duties in the evenings. This dual burden creates a sense of overload and exhaustion, as there is little time left for self-care or relaxation. The pressure to fulfill multiple roles can lead to feelings of guilt, as individuals may feel that they are not doing enough in either domain, further contributing to emotional exhaustion and burnout.

Moreover, societal expectations around resilience and stoicism often discourage individuals from acknowledging their own limitations or seeking help. In many cultures, there is a stigma around discussing mental health or admitting vulnerability, as it may be perceived as a sign of weakness. This societal pressure to remain strong and self-sufficient prevents individuals from seeking support when they need it most, leading to isolation and prolonged suffering. The lack of social support and validation further intensifies burnout, as individuals feel that they must bear the weight of their challenges alone.

Addressing lifestyle triggers and modern pressures requires a conscious effort to create balance and prioritize well-being. For digital overload, setting boundaries around screen time and engaging in "digital detox" practices can provide much-needed mental relief. Designating device-free times or areas, such as avoiding screens during meals or before bed, can help reduce cognitive fatigue and improve sleep quality. Practicing mindfulness and focusing on face-to-face interactions over virtual ones can foster a sense of connection and presence, reducing the impact of social comparison.

To improve sleep and nutrition, individuals must prioritize rest and adopt healthier dietary habits. Establishing a consistent sleep routine, reducing caffeine intake in the evening, and creating a calming pre-sleep environment can enhance sleep quality. Incorporating nutrient-dense foods into the diet, while reducing reliance on processed foods and sugars, can provide sustained energy and improve resilience against stress. Hydration and regular meals are essential for maintaining energy levels and supporting cognitive function, which is critical for coping with daily pressures.

Finally, challenging societal expectations and redefining personal standards of success can empower individuals to pursue a life aligned with their own values rather than external ideals. Embracing self-compassion and setting realistic goals can help individuals resist the pressure to constantly achieve or meet societal standards.

Seeking support from friends, family, or mental health professionals can also help individuals manage societal pressures and feel validated in their experiences. Developing a strong support network can provide a sense of community and shared understanding, allowing individuals to feel less alone in their struggles. For those in dual roles—such as balancing careers with care giving responsibilities—learning to ask for help and delegate tasks can ease the burden and prevent feelings of overwhelm.

One way to navigate societal expectations is through practicing mindfulness and self-reflection. By taking time to regularly assess personal goals, values, and priorities, individuals can develop a clearer understanding of what truly matters to them. This process helps shift the focus from external validation to intrinsic fulfillment, as individuals recognize that their worth is not defined solely by achievements or societal standards. Practicing gratitude and focusing on small accomplishments can foster a sense of contentment and reduce the need to constantly strive for more.

Additionally, establishing boundaries with social media and limiting exposure to idealized images can reduce the pressure of comparison. Unfollowing accounts that promote unrealistic standards, or curating a feed filled with positive, diverse, and authentic representations, can help mitigate the negative effects of social media on self-esteem. Engaging with content that aligns with one's values rather than external expectations fosters a more positive relationship with social media, reducing its impact on mental health and burnout.

Incorporating self-care practices into daily routines is another essential component in managing the pressures of modern life. Self-care is not simply about indulgence; it is about actively prioritizing mental, emotional, and physical well-being. Activities such as meditation, journalism, or spending time in nature provide opportunities to recharge and regain a sense of calm. Exercise, in particular, has been shown to reduce stress, improve mood, and increase energy levels. Incorporating these practices consistently can help individuals build resilience against burnout, as they have reliable tools for managing stress and maintaining balance.

In conclusion, lifestyle triggers and modern pressures—such as digital overload, lack of sleep, poor nutrition, and societal expectations—play a substantial role in contributing to burnout. While these factors are often deeply ingrained in today's fast-paced society, recognizing their impact allows individuals to make conscious choices that prioritize well-being. By setting boundaries, fostering healthy habits, challenging societal expectations, and engaging in self-care, individuals can create a balanced approach to modern life that supports resilience and reduces the risk of burnout.

Building Self-Awareness

Building self-awareness is a fundamental step in preventing and recovering from burnout. Self-awareness involves understanding one's physical, mental, and emotional states, as well as recognizing patterns in energy levels, mood, and behavior that might signal an impending state of burnout. Developing this awareness equips individuals with the tools to make conscious, proactive choices that support their well-being and resilience. In an environment where demands and stressors are often beyond one's control, self-awareness serves as a personal compass, allowing individuals to recognize when they need to pause, adjust, or seek support before burnout becomes unmanageable. Three essential strategies for cultivating self-awareness include monitoring energy levels and mood, journalism for reflection and insight, and establishing a personal warning system for burnout.

One of the most effective ways to build self-awareness is by monitoring your energy levels and mood throughout the day and week. By regularly checking in with yourself, you can develop a clearer picture of the times when you feel most energized and the circumstances that drain your energy. This process allows individuals to recognize patterns that indicate when they are operating at their best, as well as when they are overextending themselves. For example, some individuals may notice that they feel more alert and productive in the morning, while others might find that their energy peaks in the afternoon. By understanding these natural rhythms, individuals can schedule demanding tasks during their most productive periods, allowing for greater efficiency and reducing the likelihood of feeling overwhelmed.

Monitoring energy levels also involves recognizing the factors that influence fluctuations in energy and mood. Physical factors, such as diet, sleep quality, and exercise, play a significant role in determining energy levels. Emotional factors, such as relationships, work environment, and personal stressors, also impact mood and motivation. For instance, individuals may notice that after a night of poor sleep, they feel irritable and easily frustrated, while on well-rested days, they are more patient and engaged. By recognizing these connections, individuals can make adjustments to their lifestyle that support sustained energy and resilience, such as prioritizing sleep, engaging in regular physical activity, or finding moments of relaxation during the day.

To monitor energy levels and mood effectively, many people find it helpful to use tools such as energy tracking charts, apps, or simple check-ins where they rate their energy and mood on a scale (e.g., 1-10). Doing this consistently provides valuable data that can reveal patterns and trends over time. For example, if someone notices that their energy dips significantly on certain days, they can investigate potential causes, such as work meetings, deadlines, or specific activities, and consider ways to adjust their schedule accordingly. This practice of tracking empowers individuals to make informed choices about where to focus their energy, ultimately reducing stress and enhancing overall well-being.

Another valuable practice for building self-awareness is journalism for reflection and insight. Journalism offers a structured way to process thoughts, emotions, and experiences, helping individuals gain clarity and understanding about their own behavior and reactions. Unlike passive self-reflection, journalism is an active process that allows individuals to externalize their thoughts, making it easier to identify patterns, stressors, and potential areas for growth. Writing in a journal can help individuals explore how they respond to certain situations, recognize triggers for stress or frustration, and identify sources of joy or fulfillment in their lives.

One powerful journalism technique is to start each entry by answering a series of reflective questions, such as "What went well today?" "What challenged me?" and "How did I feel about these experiences?" This approach encourages individuals to focus not only on difficulties but also on positive moments, fostering a balanced perspective. By regularly documenting their experiences and emotions, individuals can track recurring themes, recognize situations that consistently lead to stress or happiness, and develop a more nuanced understanding of their inner world. Over time, journalism can help individuals recognize how they typically respond to stress, where their limits lie, and what strategies work best for managing challenging emotions.

For those new to journalism, it can be helpful to set aside a specific time each day, whether in the morning or before bed, to reflect on the day's events and personal reactions. This regular practice creates a habit of self-reflection, making it easier to maintain during periods of high stress. Additionally, journalism does not need to be lengthy or elaborate; even a few sentences each day can provide valuable insight. Over time, individuals can look back at previous entries to see how their mood, thoughts, and energy levels have evolved, offering perspective on personal growth and resilience.

Journalism for insight can also help individuals process complex emotions that they might otherwise suppress or overlook. Writing about difficult experiences or emotions allows individuals to explore these feelings in a safe, non-judgmental space, reducing the emotional burden associated with suppressing or ignoring them. For example, if someone feels frustration or resentment toward a particular situation or person, journalism allows them to examine these feelings openly and honestly, which can prevent the buildup of unprocessed emotions that may contribute to burnout. By developing this habit, individuals cultivate a greater sense of emotional awareness and resilience, as they learn to recognize and address difficult emotions rather than letting them fester.

A third strategy for building self-awareness is establishing a personal warning system for burnout. A personal warning system is a set of indicators that signal when burnout might be approaching, allowing individuals to take proactive steps to prevent it. Everyone experiences stress and exhaustion differently, so each person's warning system is unique and based on their specific patterns and vulnerabilities. By identifying early signs of burnout, individuals can implement self-care strategies, set boundaries, or seek support before reaching a state of complete exhaustion.

To create a personal warning system, individuals should begin by reflecting on past experiences of burnout or high stress and identifying the symptoms they experienced leading up to those periods. Common early signs of burnout include physical symptoms such as headaches, muscle tension, or digestive issues; emotional symptoms such as irritability, mood swings, or feelings of detachment; and behavioral symptoms such as procrastination, forgetfulness, or withdrawal from social activities. By recognizing these signs as potential indicators of burnout, individuals can develop a greater sense of control over their well-being, as they become attuned to their own early warning signs.

Once these signs have been identified, individuals can create a list of specific actions to take when they notice these symptoms arising. For instance, if someone's warning signs include feeling easily frustrated and snapping at loved ones, they might commit to setting aside time for relaxation, practicing breathing exercises, or engaging in a hobby that brings them joy. If another person notices that their warning signs include frequent headaches and insomnia, they may focus on adjusting their sleep routine, hydrating more regularly, and reducing caffeine intake. By creating a plan for addressing these symptoms, individuals can respond to their warning signs in a way that prevents them from progressing into full burnout.

An effective personal warning system also involves communicating with others about these signs and seeking support when needed. For instance, individuals might share their warning signs with close friends, family members, or colleagues who can help them recognize these symptoms if they arise. This shared awareness creates a support network that can provide encouragement, guidance, and accountability, making it easier to address burnout before it becomes severe. Open communication with loved ones about burnout warning signs can also reduce feelings of isolation, as individuals recognize that they are not alone in their challenges and have a network of people who care about their well-being.

Developing a personal warning system for burnout can empower individuals to approach stress and exhaustion with a proactive mindset rather than feeling helpless in the face of mounting demands. This system encourages individuals to view burnout prevention as an ongoing process rather than a single intervention, fostering resilience and adaptability in the face of life's inevitable challenges. By recognizing and responding to early warning signs, individuals can maintain greater control over their energy, emotions, and overall health, ultimately reducing the likelihood of reaching a state of complete burnout.

In conclusion, building self-awareness is a crucial step in preventing and recovering from burnout. By monitoring energy levels and mood, journalism for reflection and insight, and establishing a personal warning system, individuals can develop a deeper understanding of their own needs, limits, and patterns. This self-awareness serves as a foundation for making conscious choices that prioritize well-being and resilience, equipping individuals with the tools to navigate stress and challenges effectively. Through consistent self-reflection and self-care, individuals can cultivate a balanced and sustainable approach to life, reducing their risk of burnout and enhancing their overall quality of life.

Lifestyle Adjustments to Combat Burnout

Lifestyle adjustments are critical components of both preventing and recovering from burnout. By making intentional changes to support physical health, mental resilience, and emotional balance, individuals can create a foundation that better supports well-being. Burnout isn't simply the result of work demands or external pressures—it also emerges from the cumulative impact of daily habits that either nourish or deplete our capacity to handle stress. Three essential areas where lifestyle adjustments can significantly reduce burnout are sleep hygiene and restorative practices, nutrition and hydration, and physical exercise and movement. When these elements are addressed consistently, they provide the energy and resilience needed to navigate life's demands without becoming overwhelmed or exhausted.

The importance of sleep hygiene and restorative practices cannot be overstated, as sleep is essential for physical recovery, cognitive function, and emotional regulation. Sleep hygiene refers to the practices and habits that contribute to consistent, high-quality sleep, which is crucial for preventing burnout. Sleep is a time when the body repairs tissues, consolidates memories, and processes emotions, making it foundational for both mental and physical health. Yet, in today's fast-paced world, sleep is often sacrificed in favor of productivity, leading to sleep deprivation that compounds stress and impairs resilience.

Sleep deprivation has a cumulative impact on the body, leading to a variety of physical and mental health issues. Chronic lack of sleep can result in impaired cognitive function, reduced problem-solving skills, and increased sensitivity to stressors, all of which make individuals more susceptible to burnout. Moreover, sleep deprivation impacts mood and emotional stability, making it more challenging to regulate emotions and respond to challenges with patience and perspective. Over time, inadequate sleep depletes the body's resources, leaving individuals feeling physically exhausted, mentally foggy, and emotionally drained.

To improve sleep hygiene, individuals can implement several key practices. First, establishing a regular sleep schedule—going to bed and waking up at the same time each day—helps regulate the body's internal clock, or circadian rhythm. This consistency signals to the brain when it's time to sleep, making it easier to fall asleep and wake up naturally. Creating a calming pre-sleep routine, such as dimming lights, engaging in relaxation exercises, or reading, can also signal to the body that it's time to wind down. Avoiding stimulating activities, such as using electronic devices or engaging in intense discussions, at least an hour before bed can improve the quality of sleep, as the blue light emitted by screens disrupts melatonin production, a hormone that promotes sleep.

In addition to a consistent schedule, optimizing the sleep environment is crucial for restful sleep. A dark, cool, and quiet bedroom environment encourages deeper, uninterrupted sleep. Blackout curtains, white noise machines, or earplugs can help block out light and noise disturbances, creating a space that promotes rest. Choosing a comfortable mattress and pillows tailored to individual preferences and needs is equally important, as physical discomfort can disrupt sleep quality. For those who struggle with sleep due to racing thoughts or anxiety, mindfulness or breathing exercises before bed can help calm the mind, allowing for a smoother transition into sleep.

Incorporating restorative practices alongside sleep is another way to combat burnout. Restorative practices are activities that promote relaxation and help the body and mind recover from stress. These practices can include meditation, deep breathing exercises, gentle stretching, or activities like listening to calming music or spending time in nature. Engaging in these practices regularly provides moments of respite throughout the day, allowing individuals to recharge without waiting for bedtime. For example, taking short breaks during the day to practice deep breathing or progressive muscle relaxation can reduce tension and improve focus, preventing burnout from building up.

Nutrition and hydration also play a pivotal role in combating burnout by fueling the body and mind with essential nutrients and maintaining energy levels. A balanced diet provides the vitamins, minerals, and macro nutrients necessary for physical health, cognitive function, and emotional stability. When individuals are under chronic stress or facing high demands, the body's nutritional needs increase, making it crucial to consume foods that support resilience and endurance. Unfortunately, the modern diet, often high in processed foods and refined sugars, lacks the nutrient density needed to sustain long-term health and can contribute to fatigue, irritability, and cognitive decline.

Eating a balanced diet that includes a variety of whole foods—such as fruits, vegetables, lean proteins, whole grains, and healthy fats—ensures that the body receives a wide range of nutrients that support energy production, mental clarity, and immune function. For instance, foods rich in complex carbohydrates, like oats, quinoa, and sweet potatoes, provide a steady source of energy by stabilizing blood sugar levels, preventing the spikes and crashes that can lead to fatigue. Lean proteins, such as chicken, fish, and legumes, support muscle repair and are essential for the production of neurotransmitters that regulate mood and cognitive function. Healthy fats, found in foods like avocados, nuts, and olive oil, support brain health and hormone production, both of which are crucial for managing stress.

Vitamins and minerals also play specific roles in supporting mental and physical resilience. B vitamins, for example, are essential for energy production and stress management, while magnesium helps regulate the nervous system and promote relaxation. Vitamin D, often obtained through sunlight exposure and fortified foods, is associated with mood regulation and has been shown to reduce symptoms of anxiety and depression. By focusing on nutrient-dense foods, individuals can ensure that their bodies have the resources needed to handle stress, recover from exhaustion, and maintain mental clarity.

Hydration is equally important in supporting energy levels and cognitive function. Dehydration, even at mild levels, can impair concentration, reduce energy, and increase irritability, making it more challenging to manage daily stressors. Drinking enough water throughout the day helps maintain blood flow, regulate body temperature, and support the brain's ability to process information and make decisions. While the ideal amount of water varies depending on individual needs, a general guideline is to aim for at least eight 8-ounce glasses per day, with adjustments for factors like physical activity, climate, and individual preferences. Consuming hydrating foods, such as fruits and vegetables with high water content, can also contribute to overall hydration.

Avoiding excessive caffeine and sugar intake is essential for maintaining stable energy levels. While caffeine provides a temporary energy boost, consuming it in large quantities or late in the day can disrupt sleep, contributing to fatigue. Similarly, sugary snacks cause rapid blood sugar spikes followed by crashes, which can leave individuals feeling drained and unfocused. Instead, opting for small, balanced meals and snacks throughout the day helps maintain stable energy levels, preventing the need for stimulants that ultimately worsen fatigue. For those who experience stress-related digestive issues, choosing easily digestible foods, such as soups, smoothies, or cooked vegetables, can reduce discomfort and support nutrient absorption, ensuring that the body receives the fuel it needs.

The role of physical exercise and movement in promoting mental well-being and combating burnout is well-documented. Physical activity has numerous benefits, including reducing stress, improving mood, and enhancing energy levels. Exercise releases endorphins, chemicals in the brain that act as natural painkillers and mood elevators, which can alleviate symptoms of anxiety and depression associated with burnout. Regular movement also reduces levels of cortisol, the body's primary stress hormone, helping to regulate the body's response to stress and promote relaxation. Engaging in physical activity, whether through structured exercise or casual movement, provides a healthy outlet for releasing tension and processing emotions, preventing them from accumulating into burnout.

Exercise doesn't need to be intense or time-consuming to be effective. In fact, even moderate physical activity, such as walking, yoga, or dancing, can provide significant mental and physical benefits. For those who experience burnout, the thought of intense workouts may feel overwhelming, so starting with gentle forms of exercise can make movement feel more accessible and enjoyable. Walking, for example, is a low-impact activity that requires no equipment and can be done anywhere. Taking a short walk during lunch breaks or after work not only provides physical exercise but also allows for a mental break from daily responsibilities, promoting relaxation and mental clarity.

Incorporating a variety of physical activities can help prevent burnout by engaging different muscle groups, challenging the body, and keeping exercise interesting. For example, combining aerobic exercises, like cycling or swimming, with strength training or stretching practices, such as Pilates or yoga, can improve overall fitness, flexibility, and balance. Activities like yoga and tai chi, in particular, combine movement with breath work and mindfulness, which can reduce anxiety and improve self-awareness. These practices encourage individuals to focus on the present moment, releasing worries and enhancing resilience against stress.

For those who work in sedentary jobs, regular movement throughout the day is essential for preventing burnout. Sitting for prolonged periods has been associated with increased risk of health issues, including cardiovascular disease and musculoskeletal pain, both of which contribute to fatigue and stress. Simple practices, such as standing up to stretch, walking around the office, or doing desk exercises, can improve circulation and reduce stiffness. Incorporating movement into the workday helps maintain energy levels and prevents the physical discomfort associated with extended sitting, supporting both productivity and well-being.

In addition to structured exercise, engaging in enjoyable physical activities or hobbies can also contribute to mental well-being. Activities like gardening, dancing, or playing a recreational sport provide a sense of fulfillment and fun, reducing stress and adding variety to daily routines. Participating in group activities or classes can also foster a sense of community and social connection, both of which are important for mental health. These activities provide an opportunity to unwind, focus on the present, and reconnect with one's interests and passions, all of which help combat burnout and improve overall life satisfaction.

In conclusion, lifestyle adjustments—such as improving sleep hygiene, adopting a balanced diet and hydration routine, and incorporating regular movement—are powerful tools in combating burnout. By prioritizing these aspects of health, individuals can build a foundation of resilience and energy that supports them in navigating life's demands.

Sleep, nutrition, and physical activity are interdependent elements that together create a foundation for mental, physical, and emotional well-being. When individuals prioritize these lifestyle adjustments, they are better equipped to handle stress, maintain focus, and engage in life with a greater sense of balance and fulfillment. Each of these areas—sleep, nutrition, and exercise—acts as a protective buffer against the challenges and pressures of daily life. By ensuring that the body and mind are well-supported, individuals build resilience, making it less likely that they will reach the state of exhaustion and emotional depletion associated with burnout.

Consistent self-care through these lifestyle adjustments also encourages a mindset shift away from seeing well-being as secondary to productivity. It emphasizes the importance of caring for oneself as a prerequisite for sustained performance, creativity, and fulfillment. This approach challenges the traditional view that productivity requires constant output and sacrifices, helping individuals recognize that rest, nutrition, and movement are essential for long-term success. By re framing self-care as a vital component of a healthy, effective lifestyle, individuals can combat burnout not only by addressing its symptoms but also by establishing habits that prevent it from developing in the first place.

Ultimately, making lifestyle adjustments to support sleep, nutrition, and physical activity is a proactive approach to well-being that benefits every area of life. When these foundations are prioritized, individuals experience greater clarity, energy, and resilience, enabling them to approach challenges with a calm and balanced perspective. Over time, these lifestyle habits become part of a sustainable routine that nurtures both body and mind, ensuring that individuals can thrive rather than merely survive in today's demanding world.

Setting Boundaries and Prioritizing Self-Care

Setting boundaries and prioritizing self-care are two essential strategies in building resilience against burnout. In a world where demands on time, energy, and attention are constantly increasing, boundaries serve as protective limits that help individuals manage their resources effectively. Boundaries act as safeguards that preserve personal space, mental clarity, and emotional well-being, while self-care practices replenish these resources, ensuring that individuals can engage in daily life with energy and purpose. Mastering the skills of saying no, developing healthy boundaries both at work and in personal life, and adopting effective self-care techniques is crucial for maintaining balance and preventing exhaustion.

How to Say No Without Guilt

Learning to say no without guilt is a transformation skill for maintaining boundaries and preventing burnout. Many people feel obligated to agree to requests, whether from colleagues, friends, or family members, due to a sense of duty, loyalty, or fear of disappointing others. However, constantly saying yes can lead to over commitment, resulting in a depletion of time and energy and reducing the quality of work and personal engagement. When individuals say yes to everything, they unintentionally sacrifice their own well-being, ultimately becoming overwhelmed and resentful.

The first step in saying no effectively is to understand that declining a request is not inherently selfish or rude. Saying no is an act of self-respect, an acknowledgment that one's resources are finite and that managing these resources wisely is essential for overall well-being. When individuals say no, they are prioritizing tasks, activities, and commitments that align with their values and goals, enabling them to give their full attention to what truly matters. Realizing that saying no can be both respectful and necessary helps individuals let go of the guilt associated with setting limits.

A helpful approach to saying no without guilt is to practice clear, honest, and respectful communication. Rather than offering lengthy explanations or apologies, a simple, straightforward response is often the most effective. For example, if a colleague asks for assistance with a project, one might respond, "I appreciate you thinking of me, but I have other commitments that need my attention." This kind of response is polite yet firm, conveying appreciation without over-apologizing or feeling the need to justify one's decision. By maintaining clarity and brevity, individuals can assert their boundaries while remaining respectful and professional.

Another effective strategy for saying no is to offer an alternative when appropriate. If declining a request feels uncomfortable, individuals can suggest another time, recommend a different person who might be able to help, or offer to contribute in a limited capacity. For instance, one might respond to a request by saying, "I'm unable to commit fully to this right now, but I'd be happy to review it briefly if that would help." Offering alternatives allows individuals to maintain boundaries while still being supportive, which can alleviate guilt and strengthen relationships.

It can also be helpful to remember that saying no is a learned skill that improves with practice. For those who struggle with guilt, starting with small, low-stakes situations can help build confidence. By practicing saying no to minor requests or invitations, individuals can become more comfortable with the process and gradually apply this skill to more significant commitments.

Over time, setting boundaries becomes a natural part of communication, empowering individuals to protect their time and energy without feeling obligated to explain or apologize.

Developing Healthy Boundaries at Work and in Personal Life

Healthy boundaries are essential in both work and personal life, as they establish limits that prevent others from overstepping and allow individuals to focus on their own needs. Boundaries help maintain a sense of autonomy, protect against burnout, and create a balanced relationship between responsibilities and personal well-being. Without boundaries, individuals risk becoming overwhelmed, as they lack the structures needed to separate different aspects of their lives and manage their commitments effectively.

In the workplace, developing healthy boundaries involves clarifying roles, setting realistic expectations, and managing workload. One of the most effective ways to establish boundaries at work is by defining and communicating one's capacity. For example, setting clear working hours and avoiding after-hours communication helps create a separation between work and personal time, which is essential for recharging. If colleagues or supervisors expect responses outside of working hours, individuals can establish a boundary by stating, "I'm available during these hours, but I'll address any questions or concerns first thing tomorrow." This proactive communication reinforces one's availability without leaving room for ambiguity.

Setting boundaries also involves managing workload and knowing when to request additional support. If an individual feels overwhelmed with assignments or projects, openly discussing workload with a supervisor can help distribute tasks more evenly. Many people fear that asking for help or setting limits might be viewed as a lack of commitment, but communicating capacity shows that one is dedicated to delivering high-quality work without compromising well-being. Setting boundaries around workload prevents individuals from taking on more than they can handle, reducing the likelihood of burnout.

In personal life, boundaries play a similarly critical role in maintaining relationships that are healthy and fulfilling. Personal boundaries define how individuals interact with friends, family, and acquaintances, protecting their emotional well-being and preserving energy for meaningful connections. One common challenge in personal boundaries is dealing with people who expect constant availability or support. While it is natural to want to help loved ones, continually putting others' needs ahead of one's own can lead to resentment and emotional exhaustion. Setting limits, such as deciding when to be available for phone calls or visits, ensures that individuals have time to focus on their own self-care and interests.

Boundaries in personal life also apply to emotional interactions. Establishing emotional boundaries involves recognizing one's limits in terms of empathy, listening, and providing support. For instance, if a friend or family member consistently shares problems without considering the listener's emotional capacity, the listener can set a boundary by expressing that they need a break from emotionally intense conversations. One might say, "I value our friendship, but I need some time to recharge. Let's reconnect tomorrow when I can give you my full attention." This type of boundary-setting is both respectful and protective, as it prevents emotional burnout while preserving the relationship.

For those who struggle with setting boundaries, it can be helpful to reflect on personal values and priorities. By identifying what matters most, individuals can make boundary-setting decisions based on alignment with these values. For example, someone who values family time might set boundaries around work-related calls during evenings, while someone who values self-care might prioritize personal time on weekends. Aligning boundaries with values helps individuals stay consistent in their decisions, as they are guided by a clear sense of purpose rather than the fear of disappointing others.

Effective Self-Care Techniques That Fit Busy Schedules

Self-care is essential for maintaining mental, emotional, and physical health, yet many individuals struggle to find time for self-care midst busy schedules. Effective self-care techniques don't necessarily require hours of free time; even small, consistent practices can provide significant benefits. By incorporating self-care into daily routines in manageable ways, individuals can foster resilience and prevent burnout without feeling overwhelmed.

One simple but effective self-care technique is to integrate short breaks throughout the day. Taking a few minutes to step away from work, stretch, or practice deep breathing can refresh the mind and reduce stress. These breaks allow individuals to reset and return to tasks with renewed focus. Techniques such as the Pomodoro Technique, which involves working in focused intervals followed by short breaks, provide a structured approach to incorporating regular pauses. By making breaks part of a routine, individuals create moments of rest that can prevent burnout, even during busy days.

Mindfulness practices, such as meditation, breathing exercises, or mindful walking, offer another accessible form of self-care. Mindfulness doesn't require extensive time or resources; even a few minutes of deep breathing can reduce anxiety and improve mental clarity. Practicing mindfulness regularly helps individuals cultivate awareness of their emotions and reactions, allowing them to manage stress more effectively. For those who struggle to find dedicated time for meditation, incorporating mindfulness into daily activities—such as mindful eating, showering, or walking—can create moments of calm and presence.

Physical self-care, such as exercise and movement, is another important element that can be tailored to fit busy schedules. Even short bursts of physical activity, such as a 10-minute walk or a few stretches, can improve mood and energy levels. Exercise releases endorphins, which enhance mental well-being, making it a powerful tool for managing stress. For individuals with limited time, choosing enjoyable activities or combining exercise with other tasks—such as walking while listening to an audio book—can make physical self-care more sustainable.

Nourishing the body through healthy meals and hydration is also a crucial aspect of self-care that can be integrated into busy days. Preparing simple, balanced meals or keeping nutritious snacks on hand provides sustained energy and supports mental clarity. Staying hydrated is equally important, as dehydration can lead to fatigue and reduced focus. Carrying a reusable water bottle and setting reminders to drink water throughout the day are simple strategies to maintain hydration. By prioritizing nutrition and hydration, individuals ensure that their bodies are well-supported, even during demanding periods.

Creating a bedtime routine that promotes restful sleep is another effective self-care technique. Establishing a consistent sleep schedule, avoiding screens before bed, and engaging in relaxing activities can improve sleep quality and help individuals recharge. For those who struggle to unwind, reading, listening to calming music, or practicing gentle stretching can ease the transition to sleep. Quality sleep is foundational to physical and mental health, and a well-rested individual is better equipped to handle stress and avoid burnout.

Engaging in hobbies or activities that bring joy and fulfillment is another valuable form of self-care. Hobbies provide a sense of accomplishment and relaxation, allowing individuals to step away from responsibilities and focus on personal interests. Whether it's painting, gardening, cooking, or playing an instrument, hobbies foster creativity and a sense of connection with oneself. Even dedicating a small amount of time each week to a hobby can provide an outlet for stress, enhancing overall well-being.

Incorporating self-care into a busy schedule often requires planning and intention. Many individuals find it helpful to schedule self-care activities just as they would any other commitment. By blocking off time in the calendar for a walk, a favorite hobby, or even a short meditation session, self-care becomes a non-negotiable part of the day rather than something that's only considered when time permits. This proactive approach to scheduling self-care helps ensure that these activities are consistently prioritized, reinforcing the importance of personal well-being midst other responsibilities.

For those who feel pressed for time, stacking self-care practices with routine activities can also be effective. For instance, practicing gratitude while commuting, listening to calming music while preparing meals, or stretching while watching a favorite show are all ways to integrate self-care seamlessly into the day. This approach minimizes the feeling that self-care is an additional task and instead makes it a natural extension of existing routines. By embedding small moments of care into everyday activities, individuals can sustain their well-being without significantly altering their schedules.

Setting realistic self-care goals is also essential for making these practices sustainable. While lengthy meditation sessions or intensive exercise routines may be ideal for some, they are not always feasible for individuals with demanding schedules. Instead, focusing on achievable and enjoyable practices helps build a habit of self-care that feels manageable rather than burdensome. For example, committing to a five-minute stretch every morning, a quick journal entry at night, or a 10-minute walk during lunch is more attainable and less overwhelming. When self-care feels achievable, it becomes a positive and empowering experience rather than another source of stress.

Self-care is not solely an individual pursuit; it can also involve connecting with others in ways that are nourishing and supportive. Social connections play a critical role in emotional resilience, as spending time with friends, family, or support groups provides a sense of belonging and shared understanding. For busy individuals, finding ways to combine self-care with social interactions can create a balanced approach to well-being. Whether it's a quick phone call with a friend, a walk with a colleague, or a family meal, these moments of connection foster emotional support and reduce feelings of isolation, both of which are protective factors against burnout.

In sum, setting boundaries and prioritizing self-care are essential strategies for managing the demands of modern life and preventing burnout. By learning to say no without guilt, developing healthy boundaries in both professional and personal contexts, and incorporating effective self-care practices into daily routines, individuals can create a lifestyle that supports their mental, emotional, and physical well-being. This balanced approach helps individuals sustain their energy, preserve their mental clarity, and engage with life's demands with resilience and intention. Through conscious boundary-setting and small, consistent acts of self-care, individuals can safeguard their well-being, enabling them to thrive rather than merely survive in today's fast-paced world.

Building Resilience in High-Stress Jobs

In today's fast-paced and high-pressure work environments, resilience has become essential for navigating the stress and demands of high-stress jobs. Resilience isn't simply about enduring challenges but involves cultivating the mental, emotional, and behavioral flexibility needed to adapt to adversity without becoming overwhelmed. For those in demanding fields—such as healthcare, law, finance, and education—resilience is critical in managing burnout and maintaining mental well-being. Building resilience at work involves adopting mindfulness and stress reduction techniques, applying cognitive-behavioral approaches to workplace stress, and learning how to shift one's perspective on work challenges. These strategies empower individuals to respond effectively to stressors, remain engaged with their work, and sustain their energy over the long term.

Mindfulness and Stress Reduction Techniques

Mindfulness has become one of the most effective approaches for managing workplace stress and enhancing resilience. At its core, mindfulness is the practice of paying focused, non-judgmental attention to the present moment. Rather than getting caught up in worries about the future or regrets about the past, mindfulness encourages individuals to stay grounded in their current experience. This mental clarity enables individuals to respond to stress with calmness and focus rather than reacting impulsively or becoming overwhelmed. For those in high-stress jobs, mindfulness serves as a mental "pause button," allowing individuals to regain control over their reactions to challenging situations.

Mindfulness-based stress reduction (MBSR) techniques, such as deep breathing, body scans, and mindful meditation, help reduce stress by activating the body's relaxation response. When stress arises, the body's fight-or-flight response is triggered, causing physical symptoms like increased heart rate, muscle tension, and rapid breathing. By practicing mindfulness, individuals can consciously engage the parasympathetic nervous system, which counteracts this stress response and promotes relaxation. Simple practices like deep breathing—where one inhales deeply, holds the breath momentarily, and exhales slowly—can lower cortisol levels and reduce physical signs of stress in real time. Regularly practicing deep breathing or short meditation breaks throughout the workday can create a buffer against the accumulation of stress, enhancing resilience over time.

Another key benefit of mindfulness is its ability to enhance self-awareness. When individuals are mindful, they are more attuned to their own emotions, thoughts, and physical sensations, which enables them to recognize early signs of stress or burnout. For instance, a healthcare professional may notice tension in their shoulders and a racing mind during a hectic shift. By practicing mindfulness, they can identify these signs as indicators of stress and take proactive steps to manage it—perhaps through a few minutes of focused breathing or a brief pause to stretch. This heightened awareness helps prevent stress from escalating into burnout by encouraging timely self-care.

Incorporating mindfulness into the workplace doesn't require long periods of meditation or drastic changes to one's routine. Even small practices, such as taking a few moments to focus on one's breath before a meeting or engaging in mindful walking during lunch breaks, can make a meaningful difference. Organizations can also support mindfulness by creating designated quiet spaces for employees to take mental breaks or by offering mindfulness workshops or apps that provide guided meditation exercises. When mindfulness is encouraged as part of workplace culture, it creates an environment where employees feel empowered to prioritize their mental health, contributing to a more resilient and engaged workforce.

Cognitive Behavioral Approaches for Workplace Stress

Cognitive Behavioral Therapy (CBT) is a widely recognized therapeutic approach that focuses on identifying and challenging unhelpful thought patterns that contribute to stress and anxiety. Cognitive-behavioral techniques can be highly effective in managing workplace stress, as they help individuals recognize how their thoughts influence their emotions and behaviors. By becoming aware of negative or distorted thinking patterns, individuals can replace them with more balanced and constructive perspectives, thereby reducing stress and building resilience. Applying cognitive-behavioral strategies in the workplace empowers individuals to re-frame challenges, reduce self-imposed pressure, and develop healthier coping mechanisms.

One of the foundational techniques in CBT is recognizing and challenging cognitive distortions—irrational or exaggerated ways of thinking that often lead to increased stress. Common cognitive distortions in the workplace include "catastrophic" (assuming the worst-case scenario will happen), "all-or-nothing thinking" (viewing situations as entirely good or bad), and "over generalization" (drawing broad conclusions based on limited evidence). For example, an employee who makes a minor mistake on a project might immediately think, "I'm terrible at my job, and my boss will think I'm incompetent." This type of thinking fuels stress and self-doubt, which can ultimately contribute to burnout.

To counter these distortions, individuals can use techniques such as cognitive restructuring, where they identify the thought, assess its accuracy, and replace it with a more balanced perspective. In the example above, the employee might challenge their thought by asking, "Is this one mistake truly reflective of my entire performance?" and "What evidence do I have that I'm capable and competent?" By re-framing the thought in a more balanced way—such as "Mistakes happen to everyone, and I can learn from this experience"—the employee reduces stress and maintains a healthier outlook.

Another cognitive-behavioral technique for managing workplace stress is "problem-solving therapy," which encourages individuals to approach work challenges systematically rather than feeling overwhelmed. When faced with a challenging task or situation, breaking it down into manageable steps makes it less daunting and allows for more effective problem-solving. For instance, if an employee is overwhelmed by a large project, they might divide it into smaller tasks and prioritize each one based on urgency and importance. This structured approach provides a sense of control and progress, reducing anxiety and preventing feelings of helplessness.

Goal setting is also a valuable cognitive-behavioral approach that can enhance resilience in the workplace. Setting realistic, achievable goals allows individuals to focus on incremental progress rather than becoming overwhelmed by the larger picture. For example, instead of aiming to complete an entire project in one sitting, setting smaller goals—such as completing a specific section or reaching a preliminary milestone—makes the task feel more attainable. Achieving these smaller goals builds confidence, reinforces positive thinking, and reduces the sense of pressure that contributes to burnout.

Additionally, CBT techniques encourage individuals to cultivate self-compassion, which is especially valuable in high-stress jobs where mistakes are often inevitable. Instead of engaging in self-criticism, individuals can practice self-compassion by recognizing that everyone faces challenges and setbacks. This shift in perspective promotes a growth mindset, where individuals view mistakes as opportunities for learning rather than sources of self-judgment. Self-compassion reduces the stress associated with high expectations and perfectionism, helping individuals approach their work with greater resilience.

How to Shift Your Perspective on Work Challenges

One of the most effective ways to build resilience in high-stress jobs is to develop the ability to shift one's perspective on work challenges. Often, the way individuals interpret and respond to challenges determines the level of stress they experience. By adopting a growth-oriented and flexible mindset, individuals can transform challenges into opportunities for growth, reducing the negative impact of stress. Perspective-shifting is not about ignoring difficulties but rather about re-framing them in ways that foster resilience and adaptability.

One way to shift perspective on work challenges is by viewing setbacks as temporary and solvable rather than permanent or insurmountable. This concept, often referred to as having a "growth mindset," helps individuals see challenges as part of the learning process rather than as threats to their competence or self-worth. For example, if an individual faces a setback, such as receiving critical feedback on a project, they might initially feel discouraged or defensive. However, by shifting their perspective, they can view the feedback as an opportunity to improve their skills, recognizing that growth often comes from overcoming challenges.

A growth mindset also encourages individuals to focus on what they can control rather than dwelling on external factors beyond their influence. In high-stress jobs, there are often many variables—such as client demands, organizational changes, or team dynamics—that can contribute to stress. By focusing on controllable factors, such as personal effort, attitude, and time management, individuals can reduce feelings of helplessness and enhance their sense of agency. For instance, rather than feeling overwhelmed by a challenging work environment, an employee might focus on improving their time management, building supportive relationships with colleagues, or seeking additional training. This focus on controllable elements empowers individuals to take proactive steps, fostering resilience against external pressures.

Another helpful perspective shift is to view work challenges as opportunities for personal and professional development. Challenges often require individuals to step outside their comfort zones, develop new skills, and adapt to unfamiliar situations. By framing challenges as growth experiences, individuals can reduce the fear and resistance that often accompany difficult tasks. For instance, if a manager is tasked with leading a high-stakes project, they might initially feel anxious or unsure. However, by viewing the project as an opportunity to strengthen leadership skills and gain valuable experience, the manager can approach it with a sense of excitement rather than dread.

Practicing gratitude is another technique for shifting perspective on work challenges. Gratitude involves recognizing and appreciating positive aspects of one's work and environment, even in the midst of stress. For instance, reflecting on supportive colleagues, meaningful work tasks, or opportunities for advancement can help individuals feel more connected to their jobs and less consumed by negative aspects. Regularly practicing gratitude can foster a sense of fulfillment and purpose, which helps buffer against burnout. When individuals focus on what they appreciate, they build resilience by cultivating a more balanced view of their work experiences.

Finally, adopting a solution-oriented mindset can help individuals re-frame challenges as manageable problems rather than overwhelming obstacles. Instead of focusing on what's going wrong, individuals can shift their attention to potential solutions and strategies. This approach encourages proactive thinking and problem-solving, which reduces feelings of stress and empowers individuals to take action. For example, if an employee is dealing with a heavy workload, they might prioritize tasks, delegate responsibilities where possible, and communicate with supervisors about deadlines.

By focusing on solutions rather than the problem itself, individuals foster a proactive mindset that reduces feelings of helplessness and promotes confidence. This shift not only helps in managing the immediate challenge but also builds long-term resilience, as individuals learn that they have the tools and resources to tackle difficult situations.

Practicing regular self-reflection is also beneficial in helping individuals shift their perspective on work challenges. Taking time to evaluate past experiences and analyze how certain challenges were overcome reinforces confidence in one's abilities. Reflecting on previous successes, and even on failures that led to growth, enables individuals to see patterns in how they respond to stress and build resilience. This self-reflection process also helps individuals acknowledge their own progress and strengths, making it easier to approach future challenges with a constructive and solution-focused mindset.

By integrating these perspective-shifting techniques into daily routines, individuals in high-stress jobs can transform their approach to challenges, enhancing their ability to navigate demanding environments without succumbing to burnout. Adopting a growth mindset, focusing on what is within one's control, and viewing challenges as opportunities for personal and professional growth are all essential strategies that can turn stressors into experiences that reinforce resilience.

In conclusion, building resilience in high-stress jobs is a multifaceted process that involves developing mental and emotional flexibility, learning effective coping mechanisms, and shifting perspectives on workplace challenges. By incorporating mindfulness practices to manage stress in real-time, applying cognitive-behavioral approaches to reshape thought patterns, and adopting a proactive, growth-oriented perspective on challenges, individuals can navigate high-pressure environments more effectively. These resilience-building strategies not only reduce the likelihood of burnout but also enable individuals to experience greater fulfillment and satisfaction in their work, empowering them to thrive even in the face of adversity.

Communicating Effectively with Employers

Effectively communicating with employers about challenges such as burnout, workload, and work-life balance is essential for maintaining both personal well-being and professional performance. Despite the importance of addressing these issues, many employees hesitate to have these conversations out of concern for appearing uncommitted or unable to manage their responsibilities. However, open communication can not only help prevent burnout but also build trust, promote understanding, and foster a supportive work environment. By learning how to approach conversations about burnout and workload, negotiate flexible work arrangements, and seek professional support when necessary, employees can create a healthier and more balanced work experience.

How to Talk to Your Boss About Burnout and Workload

Talking to a supervisor about burnout or an overwhelming workload can feel daunting, but it's a critical step in preventing long-term issues. The first key to success in such conversations is preparation. Before approaching the topic, it's essential to clearly identify the specific challenges you're facing, as well as their impact on your well-being and productivity. Consider whether the workload is the primary issue, or if there are other contributing factors, such as lack of resources, unclear expectations, or a need for additional support. By understanding the root of the problem, you can approach the conversation with a well-defined focus, making it easier for your supervisor to understand your perspective and offer support.

When initiating a conversation about burnout, choose an appropriate time and setting. Avoid bringing it up during a high-stress period, such as just before a major deadline or during a busy team meeting, as this might distract your supervisor and reduce the effectiveness of the conversation. Instead, request a private meeting, preferably during a time when both you and your supervisor are less likely to be interrupted. Starting the conversation in a calm, neutral setting allows for open dialogue and demonstrates that you're approaching the topic professionally and thoughtfully.

During the conversation, focus on describing your experience without placing blame. For example, instead of saying, "You've given me too much work," a more constructive approach would be, "I've been feeling overwhelmed by my current workload, and I'm concerned it may be affecting my performance." This type of language takes ownership of your feelings and experiences while inviting your supervisor to consider possible solutions. Emphasize how the situation impacts your productivity and well-being rather than making it seem like a personal criticism. This approach keeps the conversation focused on finding solutions that benefit both you and the organization.

It's also helpful to come prepared with potential solutions. Rather than simply expressing frustration, demonstrate a proactive attitude by suggesting adjustments that could alleviate the pressure. For example, you could ask for additional resources, propose redistributing certain tasks among the team, or suggest adjusting deadlines to create a more manageable workload. By offering solutions, you show your supervisor that you're committed to fulfilling your responsibilities and that you're thinking strategically about how to do so effectively. Supervisors are generally more receptive to these conversations when they see that the employee is motivated to find productive ways to address the issue.

In addition, be transparent about any specific symptoms or signs of burnout that you're experiencing, such as difficulty focusing, reduced motivation, or physical exhaustion. While it may feel uncomfortable to share these details, being open about the impact of burnout can help your supervisor understand the urgency of the situation. However, avoid overwhelming them with too many personal details; focus instead on explaining how the symptoms are affecting your work and your ability to meet expectations. Providing this context makes it clear that burnout is not just a personal issue but one that directly impacts your performance, which is likely to prompt a more supportive response.

Finally, approach the conversation with a collaborative mindset. Instead of expecting your supervisor to solve the issue independently, frame the discussion as an opportunity to work together to create a sustainable solution. By emphasizing teamwork and shared goals, you're more likely to build a relationship based on mutual respect and support. Supervisors who feel engaged in the solution process are often more committed to helping employees achieve a manageable workload and maintain well-being.

Negotiating Flexible Work Arrangements

Flexible work arrangements have become increasingly common as companies recognize the value of supporting work-life balance. For employees facing burnout or juggling competing responsibilities, negotiating flexible work arrangements can provide the balance needed to reduce stress and enhance productivity. Flexibility can take various forms, including remote work, flexible hours, compressed workweeks, or job-sharing. Successfully negotiating a flexible arrangement requires careful preparation, clear communication, and an understanding of both your needs and your employer's priorities.

Before initiating a request for flexibility, evaluate your own goals and limitations. Consider how different arrangements might improve your work-life balance, productivity, and well-being. For example, if you find that long commutes are exhausting or if your work involves tasks that require deep focus, remote work or flexible hours might provide the mental space needed to work more effectively. On the other hand, if family responsibilities are a significant factor, flexible hours or a compressed workweek might help you manage both personal and professional commitments more effectively.

Once you've identified the arrangement that would be most beneficial, prepare a proposal that outlines your request in detail. Your proposal should include the specific changes you're requesting, the rationale behind your request, and how the arrangement will enable you to fulfill your responsibilities more effectively. For example, if you're requesting to work remotely two days a week, explain how this arrangement would reduce burnout by allowing you to rest on non-commute days, ultimately enhancing your focus and productivity. Including concrete examples of how flexibility will benefit both you and the organization helps strengthen your case.

When discussing flexible arrangements with your employer, emphasize how the change aligns with your commitment to productivity and achieving organizational goals. Employers are more likely to approve flexible arrangements when they understand that these adjustments will support, rather than hinder, your performance. For instance, you might say, "Working from home twice a week would allow me to focus on tasks that require concentration, which I believe will improve the quality of my work." By framing your request as a way to enhance productivity, you demonstrate that your priority is the organization's success, not just personal convenience.

It's also helpful to anticipate potential concerns and come prepared with solutions. Supervisors may worry that flexible arrangements will disrupt team dynamics or create challenges in communication. Address these concerns proactively by proposing solutions, such as setting specific "office hours" for communication or scheduling regular check-ins to maintain team cohesion. By showing that you've thought through how to address potential obstacles, you make it easier for your supervisor to envision how flexibility could work smoothly in your role.

If your request is met with resistance, consider proposing a trial period. A temporary arrangement, such as a three-month trial, allows both you and your employer to evaluate whether the flexibility benefits productivity and well-being. At the end of the trial, you can review the arrangement together, discussing what worked, what didn't, and whether any adjustments are needed. This approach reduces the perceived risk for your employer and demonstrates your willingness to adapt based on what works best for both parties.

In cases where traditional flexibility options are not feasible, explore alternative solutions that may offer similar benefits. For example, if your employer cannot accommodate remote work, consider requesting flexible start and end times or designated focus hours where meetings are minimized. Flexibility doesn't have to mean complete autonomy; even small adjustments to how work is structured can make a meaningful difference in reducing stress and enhancing resilience.

Seeking Professional Support: When and How to Ask

Recognizing when to seek professional support—whether it's from a mental health provider, employee assistance program (EAP), or HR department—is an important part of managing burnout and maintaining well-being at work. Professional support can provide employees with resources, strategies, and validation that help them navigate challenges more effectively. While it can be intimidating to reach out for help, seeking support is a proactive choice that prioritizes health and resilience. Understanding when and how to ask for help can make the process smoother and less daunting.

The first step in seeking professional support is recognizing when personal strategies for managing stress and burnout are no longer sufficient. Signs that it may be time to seek additional help include persistent exhaustion, difficulty concentrating, feelings of hopelessness, or physical symptoms like headaches or insomnia that do not improve with lifestyle adjustments. If burnout is affecting your mental health, personal relationships, or overall quality of life, professional support can provide a valuable perspective and introduce more structured coping strategies.

If your workplace offers an Employee Assistance Program (EAP), consider reaching out for confidential guidance. EAPs are often underutilized but can offer free resources such as counseling sessions, workshops, and mental health assessments. Contacting the EAP is typically confidential, and the support provided can range from emotional counseling to practical advice on managing workload and improving time management. Many EAPs also offer referrals to external mental health providers, allowing employees to continue receiving support beyond the initial sessions.

When approaching HR for support, it's helpful to focus on specific needs or accommodations that could alleviate burnout. For example, if workload management or flexibility would help reduce stress, express your needs in terms of practical adjustments rather than general complaints. An HR professional can provide insights into available resources, such as mental health days, wellness programs, or adjustments in workload distribution. Discussing burnout with HR can also create a sense of accountability and enable HR to track and address trends related to employee well-being, fostering a healthier workplace culture over time.

If you're seeking external professional support, such as therapy or counseling, research local providers or consider virtual therapy options. Many therapists specialize in workplace stress and burnout, providing strategies to manage pressure, set boundaries, and improve emotional resilience. For individuals who are uncertain about how to get started, a primary care physician or mental health advocate can help with referrals or recommendations based on specific needs.

When discussing burnout or mental health concerns with a professional, it's essential to be open and honest about your experiences. Provide specific examples of how burnout is affecting your life, such as difficulties at work, emotional strain, or physical symptoms.

This transparency allows the professional to gain a clear understanding of your situation and offer targeted support. For example, a counselor might provide techniques to manage stress in real time, such as grounding exercises or cognitive re-framing, while a therapist could help you explore deeper issues related to perfectionism, self-criticism, or boundary-setting. By openly sharing your challenges, you enable the professional to tailor their approach, ensuring the guidance provided is relevant to your needs.

It's important to remember that seeking professional support is a proactive step, not a sign of weakness. Many people hesitate to reach out for help because they fear judgment or believe they should be able to handle challenges independently. However, workplace burnout is a widespread issue that impacts individuals across industries and positions. Asking for support when it's needed is an acknowledgment of your commitment to well-being and to maintaining your effectiveness at work. Engaging with professional support can provide fresh perspectives, coping strategies, and validation, all of which contribute to building resilience and preventing burnout from worsening.

For those who feel unsure about how to bring up mental health with their employers, practicing the conversation beforehand can be helpful. Prepare a brief outline of what you want to discuss, focusing on the challenges you're facing, their impact on your performance, and any solutions you're seeking. You may choose to bring up specific aspects of your work environment that are contributing to burnout, such as high workload, lack of resources, or conflicting priorities. Framing the conversation around workplace improvements rather than solely on personal issues can make it easier to approach and may elicit a more supportive response from employers.

In some cases, employees may be eligible for workplace accommodations if burnout or mental health concerns significantly impact their ability to perform. Under laws such as the Americans with Disabilities Act (ADA), individuals with mental health conditions that limit major life activities may be entitled to reasonable accommodations, such as modified work schedules, reduced hours, or access to quiet workspace. If accommodations could benefit your mental health and reduce burnout, HR can guide you through the process of formally requesting these adjustments. Engaging in an open conversation about your needs and available accommodations can help create a work environment that supports both your well-being and productivity.

In conclusion, communicating effectively with employers about burnout, workload, and flexible arrangements is an essential skill for maintaining balance and resilience in today's demanding work environments. By preparing thoughtfully, approaching conversations with clarity and confidence, and seeking professional support when needed, employees can navigate workplace challenges in a way that promotes both personal well-being and professional success. Through open and constructive communication, individuals not only reduce the risk of burnout but also contribute to a more supportive and understanding workplace culture, benefiting both themselves and their organizations.

Creating a Supportive Work Environment

A supportive work environment is critical for employee well-being, engagement, and productivity. In today's fast-paced, high-demand work culture, burnout has become a pervasive issue, affecting both individual employees and the organization as a whole. Burnout not only diminishes employee satisfaction and engagement but also leads to decreased productivity, higher turnover rates, and increased healthcare costs. To mitigate these effects and foster a workplace where employees feel valued and empowered, organizations must actively cultivate a supportive work environment. This involves managers playing a pivotal role in reducing burnout, encouraging team-building and collaboration, and implementing systems for meaningful recognition and rewards.

How Managers Can Reduce Employee Burnout

Managers are central to creating a work environment that reduces burnout and promotes well-being. Their attitudes, actions, and leadership styles significantly influence employee morale, job satisfaction, and stress levels. When managers are proactive about employee well-being, they set the tone for a healthier and more balanced workplace. To reduce burnout, managers should adopt a range of strategies, from workload management to fostering open communication.

One of the primary ways managers can prevent burnout is by actively monitoring and managing workloads. When employees are consistently overworked, stress levels rise, and burnout becomes more likely. Managers should ensure that workloads are balanced, achievable, and aligned with each team member's skills and strengths. Regular one-on-one meetings with employees provide an opportunity for managers to check in on workload, address any concerns, and offer support when necessary. During these meetings, managers can assess whether employees are feeling overwhelmed and, if so, explore ways to adjust responsibilities, redistribute tasks, or extend deadlines to alleviate pressure. This approach shows employees that their well-being is a priority and that they have a voice in managing their workload.

Effective managers also encourage open communication, where employees feel safe expressing concerns, seeking support, or discussing challenges without fear of judgment. Creating a culture of transparency allows employees to bring up issues related to stress or burnout early, before they escalate. Managers can foster open communication by being approachable, listening actively, and responding with empathy. When employees feel heard and understood, they are more likely to feel comfortable discussing workload or well-being concerns, making it easier for managers to intervene early and offer appropriate support.

Providing opportunities for growth and development is another essential strategy for reducing burnout. Employees who feel stagnant or unchallenged are more likely to experience disengagement, which can contribute to burnout. By offering professional development opportunities, such as training programs, workshops, or mentorship, managers enable employees to enhance their skills, build confidence, and pursue career growth. This sense of progress and accomplishment counteracts feelings of stagnation and fosters a more engaged and motivated workforce. Additionally, when employees are supported in developing new skills, they are better equipped to handle challenges, adapt to changes, and approach their roles with a renewed sense of purpose.

Flexibility is also crucial in helping employees balance work and personal responsibilities. Managers who support flexible work arrangements—such as remote work, flexible hours, or compressed workweeks—provide employees with the autonomy to manage their schedules according to their individual needs. Flexible work arrangements can reduce commuting stress, allow for better work-life balance, and support employees in managing responsibilities outside of work. By empowering employees with control over their schedules, managers show respect for employees' personal lives, reducing burnout and enhancing overall job satisfaction.

Finally, managers play a key role in setting realistic expectations and clarifying priorities. When employees are faced with multiple competing demands, they may feel pressured to complete all tasks simultaneously, leading to stress and decreased quality of work. Managers can alleviate this pressure by helping employees prioritize tasks, identifying which projects are most urgent, and providing clear guidance on deadlines and expectations. This approach not only reduces stress but also enables employees to focus on producing high-quality work, leading to greater job satisfaction and less burnout.

Team-Building and Collaboration for Reduced Stress

Team-building and fostering collaboration are essential components of a supportive work environment. When employees feel connected to their colleagues and engaged in a collaborative culture, they are more likely to experience a sense of belonging, camaraderie, and mutual support. These positive connections create a buffer against stress and provide a support network that employees can rely on during challenging times. Effective team-building and collaboration also encourage open communication, trust, and respect, making it easier for employees to navigate workplace challenges together.

Team-building activities, whether formal or informal, can strengthen relationships among team members and create a positive workplace culture. Formal team-building exercises, such as retreats, workshops, or team challenges, provide structured opportunities for employees to work together, solve problems, and build trust. These activities promote teamwork and encourage employees to leverage each other's strengths, leading to stronger collaboration on projects and daily tasks. Informal team-building activities, such as group lunches, after-work gatherings, or shared hobbies, also foster a sense of community and belonging, reducing isolation and building friendships within the team.

Creating a collaborative culture also involves encouraging open communication and mutual support among team members. Managers can set the tone for collaboration by modeling supportive behaviors, such as actively listening to team members, acknowledging diverse perspectives, and encouraging employees to share ideas. When employees feel that their contributions are valued and that they are working toward shared goals, they are more likely to collaborate effectively and to support one another in achieving common objectives. Collaboration reduces individual stress, as employees can rely on each other's expertise, share responsibilities, and tackle complex tasks as a team rather than in isolation.

Cross-functional collaboration is another valuable strategy for reducing stress and fostering a supportive environment. By encouraging employees to work across departments or with colleagues from different areas of expertise, organizations create opportunities for employees to learn from one another, expand their skill sets, and build networks within the company. This collaborative approach enables employees to broaden their understanding of the organization and gain insights into how their roles contribute to larger goals, promoting a sense of purpose and fulfillment.

Mentorship and peer support programs further enhance collaboration and create a workplace culture where employees feel supported. Mentorship allows experienced employees to guide and support newer or less experienced colleagues, providing advice, encouragement, and practical insights. Peer support programs, where employees can seek advice or share experiences with colleagues facing similar challenges, offer an additional layer of support. These programs not only foster learning and growth but also create connections that reduce isolation and build resilience, helping employees navigate stress and stay engaged.

Importance of Recognition and Reward

Recognition and reward are fundamental to creating a supportive work environment. When employees feel valued for their contributions, they experience a sense of accomplishment, satisfaction, and motivation. Recognizing and rewarding employees' efforts, achievements, and dedication reinforces their connection to the organization and boosts morale, helping to counteract the effects of burnout. A culture of recognition fosters a positive work environment where employees feel appreciated and motivated to perform at their best.

Recognition can take many forms, from formal awards and bonuses to informal expressions of appreciation. Public recognition, such as praising employees during team meetings, acknowledging achievements in company newsletters, or celebrating milestones, allows employees to feel seen and valued by the organization. Private recognition, such as a personal note or one-on-one acknowledgment from a manager, can be equally impact, as it demonstrates that the manager recognizes the individual's contributions on a personal level. Both types of recognition help employees feel that their efforts are meaningful and that their hard work is appreciated.

Managers should also provide regular, constructive feedback as part of the recognition process. Positive feedback reinforces good performance and motivates employees to continue their efforts, while constructive feedback helps employees identify areas for improvement and grow professionally. By providing consistent and balanced feedback, managers show that they are invested in employees' success and development, strengthening the relationship between employees and leadership. This supportive approach builds trust and encourages employees to seek feedback, ask for guidance, and take ownership of their growth.

Financial rewards, such as bonuses, raises, or performance-based incentives, are also effective in demonstrating appreciation and motivating employees. When employees are compensated fairly and rewarded for their achievements, they feel valued and recognized for their contributions, which reduces feelings of dissatisfaction and disengagement. Organizations should strive to create transparent and equitable reward systems, where employees understand the criteria for recognition and are aware of how their contributions directly impact their rewards. This transparency fosters trust and ensures that rewards are seen as fair, reinforcing a sense of belonging and motivation.

Non-monetary rewards, such as additional time off, flexible schedules, or professional development opportunities, also play an important role in supporting employee well-being. Offering rewards that enhance work-life balance, such as extra paid time off or remote work options, shows that the organization values employees' personal lives and understands the importance of rest and recovery. Providing opportunities for growth, such as access to training programs or tuition reimbursement, empowers employees to develop their skills and advance their careers, which contributes to long-term job satisfaction and engagement.

Creating a culture of recognition extends beyond individual rewards; it also involves fostering an environment where team achievements are celebrated. Recognizing team successes, such as completing a challenging project or achieving departmental goals, reinforces a collaborative mindset and highlights the value of collective effort. When employees see that their teamwork is appreciated, they are more likely to remain engaged, support their colleagues, and approach future challenges with enthusiasm. Celebrating team accomplishments fosters a sense of unity and shared purpose, reducing stress and building resilience within the team.

In conclusion, creating a supportive work environment requires intentional efforts by both managers and organizations to reduce employee burnout, promote collaboration, and implement systems of recognition and reward. Managers can play a critical role in preventing burnout by actively managing workloads, fostering open communication, and supporting flexibility. Team-building and collaboration create a culture of mutual support, while meaningful recognition and rewards demonstrate that employees' contributions are valued. By prioritizing these elements, organizations cultivate a positive and inclusive workplace where employees feel empowered, appreciated, and motivated, ultimately contributing to greater engagement, productivity, and overall well-being.

Rediscovering Passion and Purpose

Moving from burnout to balance is not simply about recovering energy or reducing stress; it's a transformation process that involves reconnecting with one's passions and redefining purpose. Burnout often leaves individuals feeling disconnected, unmotivated, and questioning the meaning of their work and personal lives. To truly move beyond burnout and create a balanced life, individuals need to engage in a deep reassessment of their career goals, personal values, and life priorities. This process involves finding joy in everyday moments and setting new, intentional priorities that align with a sense of fulfillment and long-term well-being. Rediscovering passion and purpose helps create a life that is not only manageable but also deeply meaningful.

Reassessing Career Goals and Personal Values

Burnout often forces individuals to confront whether their career goals and personal values are aligned. The intense fatigue and detachment that accompany burnout can signal a deeper dissatisfaction with one's professional life or current trajectory. For some, burnout is the result of pursuing goals that no longer resonate with their personal values, leading to a disconnect between what they do and what they truly care about. To move from burnout to balance, it's essential to take time for reflection and reassessment.

The first step in this process is to evaluate current career goals and how they relate to your personal values and passions. Consider what originally drew you to your career and whether those motivations still hold true. Ask yourself questions like: Why did I choose this path? What aspects of my work do I find fulfilling? What aspects drain me or feel misaligned with my values? This type of introspection allows you to identify whether burnout stems from the nature of your work, the work environment, or a misalignment between your career and personal growth.

If you find that your current career goals no longer align with your values, it may be time to redefine your professional path. This doesn't necessarily mean changing careers altogether; sometimes, a shift in responsibilities, focus, or perspective can reignite passion. For example, someone in a high-stress managerial role might find more fulfillment in a mentoring or consulting position, where they can use their expertise to help others grow without the constant pressure of day-to-day management. Alternatively, for those who feel disconnected from their work, seeking opportunities to engage in projects that align with their passions—such as volunteering, taking on new responsibilities, or developing new skills—can reignite motivation and enthusiasm.

Additionally, it's crucial to assess whether the work environment supports your values and goals. Even if the job itself aligns with your interests, a toxic or supportive workplace can lead to burnout. Consider whether the culture, leadership, and work dynamics are conducive to your personal growth and well-being. If they are not, it may be worth exploring options such as transferring to a different department, seeking a new position within the organization, or transitioning to a new company altogether.

Throughout this reassessment process, it's important to remain open to change. Shifting career goals or redefining one's path can be daunting, especially when fear of the unknown or financial stability is involved. However, staying in a situation that leads to burnout and emotional exhaustion has long-term consequences that extend beyond the professional sphere. Taking small steps toward change, such as upskilling, networking, or seeking mentorship, can create a sense of progress and build the confidence needed to make more significant shifts over time.

Finding Joy in Small Moments

Rediscovering passion and purpose also involves learning to find joy in small, everyday moments. Burnout often leads to a focus on stress, fatigue, and obligations, overshadowing the simple pleasures that can provide relief and happiness. Shifting focus to these small moments can help individuals reconnect with what makes them feel alive, engaged, and content.

One effective way to cultivate this mindset is through the practice of mindfulness, which encourages individuals to be fully present and appreciative of the current moment. Mindfulness can be as simple as taking a few minutes each day to notice your surroundings, appreciate a cup of coffee, or focus on your breath. By slowing down and savoring small experiences, you create space to reconnect with yourself and the world around you. This practice can also help shift your attention away from stressors, allowing for a more balanced perspective and reducing the intensity of burnout symptoms.

Engaging in activities that bring pleasure, no matter how small, is another powerful way to reconnect with joy. These activities don't need to be grand or time-consuming; even simple actions like reading a book, taking a walk in nature, cooking a favorite meal, or spending quality time with loved ones can provide a sense of fulfillment and happiness. By making time for these moments and treating them as essential parts of your day, you prioritize self-care and well-being over the relentless pursuit of productivity. This shift in focus from "doing" to "being" helps create balance and allows you to find joy outside of professional achievements or obligations.

Journalism about daily positive experiences is another technique for cultivating joy and gratitude. Writing about moments that bring happiness, whether it's a kind gesture from a friend, a successful outcome at work, or a beautiful sunset, helps shift focus from stress to positivist. Reflecting on these moments reinforces a sense of appreciation for the small things and encourages a habit of noticing and valuing joy. Over time, this practice can improve overall mood, reduce stress, and foster a greater sense of fulfillment, all of which are essential for overcoming burnout.

Moreover, cultivating connections with others is vital for finding joy in daily life. Burnout often isolates individuals, making it difficult to engage meaningfully with those around them. Reconnecting with friends, family, or colleagues—whether through shared activities, meaningful conversations, or simple moments of laughter—can bring a renewed sense of belonging and happiness. Social support not only provides comfort but also allows individuals to share their experiences and feel understood. Building and nurturing these connections fosters emotional resilience and reduces the impact of stress, contributing to a more balanced and joyful life.

Setting New Life Priorities

Moving from burnout to balance requires a re-evaluation of life priorities and a commitment to living in alignment with one's core values. Burnout often occurs when there is a disconnect between what individuals prioritize and what they truly value. For example, prioritizing work over personal well-being, relationships, or hobbies may lead to burnout if those sacrifices do not align with one's long-term values and goals. By setting new life priorities that reflect a deeper understanding of personal values, individuals can create a life that feels fulfilling and balanced.

The process of setting new priorities begins with identifying your core values and what matters most to you. Consider what aspects of life give you the most joy, fulfillment, and meaning. Is it spending time with loved ones, pursuing creative projects, advancing in your career, traveling, or contributing to your community? Reflect on how your current lifestyle aligns—or doesn't align—with these values. If you notice a disconnect, such as a lack of time for family or personal growth due to work demands, it may be time to shift your priorities to create a more balanced and meaningful life.

Once you have identified your values, setting specific, intentional goals is crucial for aligning your life with these priorities. For example, if building stronger relationships is a priority, set goals such as scheduling regular time with family and friends, planning meaningful activities together, or engaging in community events. If self-care and well-being are values you want to prioritize, create routines that include exercise, meditation, or hobbies that nourish your mind and body. By setting concrete goals that align with your values, you create a road map that guides your actions and decisions, making it easier to stay true to what matters most.

To ensure that these new priorities remain central in your life, it's important to establish boundaries that protect your time and energy. This may involve saying no to additional work responsibilities, setting limits on screen time, or blocking off time each week for personal or family activities. Boundaries are essential for maintaining balance and preventing the burnout that arises from overextending oneself in pursuit of external expectations. When you establish and maintain boundaries, you signal to yourself and others that your well-being and personal priorities are just as important as professional obligations.

Reassessing life priorities also involves being flexible and open to change. As you evolve and grow, your values and goals may shift, and it's important to adapt your priorities accordingly. This might mean embracing new interests, adjusting career goals, or reevaluating relationships that no longer serve your well-being. Regularly checking in with yourself—through practices like journalism, self-reflection, or discussions with trusted friends or mentors—ensures that your priorities remain aligned with your current values and passions. This ongoing process of reassessment helps prevent burnout by keeping your life dynamic and aligned with what truly matters.

Finding balance doesn't mean avoiding all challenges or stressors; it means creating a life where your efforts are directed toward goals that fulfill and energize you. By focusing on what you're passionate about and setting priorities that align with your values, you cultivate a sense of purpose and engagement that makes it easier to navigate obstacles without feeling overwhelmed. When your actions and decisions are guided by a clear understanding of your values, you build resilience and motivation, which are essential for maintaining balance and preventing burnout in the long term.

In conclusion, rediscovering passion and purpose is a transformation journey that moves individuals from burnout to balance. Through reassessing career goals and values, finding joy in small moments, and setting new life priorities that align with one's core values, individuals can create a more meaningful, fulfilling, and balanced life. This process not only addresses the symptoms of burnout but also builds a foundation for lasting well-being and resilience. By living in alignment with their passions and values, individuals can experience a renewed sense of purpose and joy, making it possible to thrive even midst life's inevitable challenges.

Maintaining Long-Term Balance

Achieving balance is not a one-time event; it is an ongoing process that requires continuous effort and adjustment. Maintaining long-term balance involves developing a resilient mindset, embracing a commitment to continuous learning and growth, and creating sustainable habits that support lasting well-being. It's about integrating practices into daily life that promote resilience, adaptability, and fulfillment, ensuring that the balance achieved can withstand the inevitable challenges and changes life brings. By cultivating these key components, individuals can build a strong foundation for long-term health, happiness, and professional success.

Developing a Resilient Mindset

A resilient mindset is essential for maintaining balance over the long term. Resilience is the ability to adapt and bounce back from adversity, and it enables individuals to face stressors and challenges without becoming overwhelmed or losing sight of their goals. Developing resilience involves cultivating a mindset that embraces change, remains flexible in the face of uncertainty, and views setbacks as opportunities for growth rather than insurmountable obstacles.

One of the core components of a resilient mindset is the ability to reframe challenges. This involves viewing difficult situations not as threats or failures but as opportunities for learning and development. When individuals experience stress or setbacks, their natural response may be to focus on the negative aspects or feel defeated. However, by consciously re-framing these experiences, individuals can shift their perspective and focus on what they can learn or how they can grow. For example, a challenging project at work might initially feel overwhelming, but by viewing it as a chance to develop new skills or demonstrate leadership, it becomes an opportunity rather than a source of stress. This shift in mindset not only reduces the emotional impact of challenges but also builds confidence and adaptability, key traits for long-term balance.

Another important aspect of resilience is developing self-compassion. Resilience does not mean ignoring or suppressing difficult emotions; it means acknowledging them with kindness and understanding. Practicing self-compassion involves treating oneself with the same care and support that one would offer a friend. When individuals face setbacks or stress, instead of criticizing themselves for feeling overwhelmed, they can practice self-compassion by recognizing that it is a natural human experience and offering themselves encouragement. Research shows that self-compassion reduces anxiety and increases emotional resilience, making it easier to recover from stressful events and maintain balance over time.

Goal-setting is also integral to a resilient mindset. Setting realistic, achievable goals provides a sense of direction and purpose, which are essential for maintaining motivation and balance. When individuals set short-term and long-term goals that align with their values and aspirations, they create a road map for growth and fulfillment. However, it's important to remain flexible in goal-setting, as circumstances may change. Resilient individuals adapt their goals as needed, adjusting their strategies when challenges arise or when priorities shift. This flexibility prevents burnout by allowing for change and growth without the pressure of rigid expectations.

Building a support network is another key factor in developing resilience. Individuals with strong social connections—whether through family, friends, colleagues, or mentors—are more likely to navigate stress successfully and maintain balance. Support networks provide emotional encouragement, practical assistance, and a sense of belonging, all of which are protective factors against burnout. Engaging with others, sharing experiences, and seeking advice create a community of support that can help individuals manage challenges more effectively. Fostering these connections requires ongoing effort, but the investment pays off by providing the social and emotional resources needed for long-term resilience.

Continuous Learning and Growth

Embracing a mindset of continuous learning and growth is vital for maintaining balance and adapting to life's changes. In a rapidly evolving world, those who are open to learning and growth are better equipped to manage new challenges, develop skills, and maintain fulfillment in both their professional and personal lives. Continuous learning is not limited to formal education; it includes developing skills, exploring interests, and seeking opportunities for self-improvement that enhance well-being and adaptability.

One way to incorporate continuous learning is through professional development. Whether it's attending workshops, pursuing certifications, or seeking mentorship opportunities, professional growth keeps individuals engaged and motivated. Expanding one's skills not only enhances career prospects but also contributes to a sense of accomplishment and purpose. When individuals feel that they are evolving and progressing in their careers, they are more likely to remain satisfied and balanced, even when faced with challenges. Professional development also builds confidence, as individuals become more competent and capable in their roles, which reduces the stress associated with uncertainty.

However, continuous learning extends beyond the professional sphere. Personal growth is equally important for maintaining balance and fulfillment. Exploring new hobbies, engaging in creative activities, or taking up interests that have been set aside due to work demands can provide a sense of renewal and joy. For instance, learning a new language, playing a musical instrument, or practicing a sport can offer a break from routine, stimulate the mind, and enhance overall well-being. Engaging in activities that promote growth outside of work allows individuals to cultivate a well-rounded life, reducing the likelihood of burnout that comes from focusing solely on professional achievements.

Lifelong learning also involves developing emotional intelligence and self-awareness. By regularly reflecting on one's thoughts, behaviors, and emotions, individuals can identify patterns that may contribute to stress or imbalance. Practicing mindfulness and meditation, for example, can help increase self-awareness and allow individuals to manage their emotions more effectively. Mindfulness practices encourage a state of presence and acceptance, helping individuals observe their thoughts and feelings without judgment. This increased awareness promotes a deeper understanding of oneself and one's needs, leading to better decision-making and the ability to adapt habits and behaviors to maintain balance.

Additionally, seeking opportunities for growth through feedback and mentorship is essential for maintaining long-term balance. Constructive feedback allows individuals to identify areas for improvement and to gain insight into how they are perceived by others. Embracing feedback as a tool for growth, rather than viewing it as criticism, builds resilience and a willingness to adapt. Mentorship, whether formal or informal, provides a supportive space for learning and growth, as mentors can offer guidance, share experiences, and provide encouragement. By seeking and valuing feedback and mentorship, individuals create a continuous cycle of growth that enhances their ability to navigate challenges and remain balanced.

Creating Sustainable Habits for Lasting Well-being

Sustainable habits are the cornerstone of long-term balance. Developing consistent, healthy routines that support physical, mental, and emotional well-being is crucial for preventing burnout and ensuring that balance can be maintained over time. The key to creating sustainable habits is to start small, be consistent, and gradually build upon these habits as they become ingrained in daily life.

Physical well-being is fundamental for long-term balance, as it directly impacts energy levels, mood, and resilience. Regular exercise, sufficient sleep, and balanced nutrition are essential habits that support overall health. Physical activity, even in moderate forms like walking, yoga, or cycling, releases endorphins that reduce stress and improve mood. Incorporating movement into daily routines can prevent the buildup of tension and provide a regular outlet for stress. Likewise, prioritizing sleep and establishing a consistent sleep schedule is vital for restoring the body and mind. Quality sleep improves cognitive function, emotional regulation, and energy levels, all of which are necessary for maintaining balance and resilience.

Nutrition also plays a significant role in sustaining well-being. Eating a balanced diet rich in whole foods, lean proteins, and healthy fats provides the nutrients needed to support physical health, cognitive function, and mood stability. Developing habits such as meal planning, staying hydrated, and avoiding excessive caffeine or processed foods helps maintain steady energy levels throughout the day, reducing fatigue and improving focus. When individuals make nutrition a priority, they equip themselves with the fuel needed to handle life's demands more effectively.

In addition to physical habits, emotional and mental well-being practices are crucial for maintaining balance. Stress management techniques, such as mindfulness, deep breathing, or journalism, provide tools for managing emotions and reducing anxiety. Integrating these practices into daily routines—whether through a morning meditation session, a brief breathing exercise during lunch, or a reflective journalism practice before bed—helps create a foundation for emotional resilience. These habits encourage self-reflection, provide moments of calm, and allow individuals to process their experiences in a healthy and constructive way.

Another key aspect of creating sustainable habits is setting boundaries. Boundaries protect one's time, energy, and mental space, ensuring that responsibilities and external demands do not overwhelm personal well-being. This may involve setting limits on work hours, establishing non-negotiable times for self-care, or communicating with others about availability and expectations. Setting and maintaining boundaries not only reduces stress but also reinforces a commitment to personal priorities. When individuals consistently uphold boundaries, they create a balance between professional and personal life that supports long-term well-being.

Social connection is also an important habit for lasting well-being. Building and nurturing relationships with friends, family, and colleagues provides emotional support, reduces isolation, and creates a sense of belonging. Making time for meaningful social interactions, whether through shared activities, conversations, or community involvement, helps individuals feel connected and supported. When social support is integrated as a consistent part of life, it serves as a buffer against stress and a resource during challenging times.

Finally, the key to sustaining these habits is flexibility and adaptability. Life's circumstances are ever-changing, and maintaining balance requires the ability to adjust habits as needed. This might mean modifying exercise routines when schedules become busier, finding alternative ways to connect with loved ones during periods of physical distance, or exploring new stress management techniques as needs evolve. Flexibility ensures that habits remain relevant and effective, allowing individuals to maintain balance even as life's demands shift.

In conclusion, maintaining long-term balance involves developing a resilient mindset, committing to continuous learning and growth, and creating sustainable habits that support well-being. By building these elements into daily life, individuals create a foundation that allows them to navigate challenges with flexibility and strength, ensuring that balance is not just achieved temporarily but maintained as a lasting, integral part of their lives.

Conclusion

The journey of managing burnout and finding balance is an ongoing, transformation process that requires self-awareness, intentionality, and adaptability. Burnout is not merely a temporary phase of exhaustion or dissatisfaction; it is a multifaceted state that affects one's mental, physical, and emotional well-being. The path to recovery and balance involves much more than simply taking a break or reducing workload; it necessitates a holistic re-evaluation of life's priorities, values, and habits. It is about understanding the root causes of burnout, implementing practical strategies to manage stress, and fostering a lifestyle that supports long-term well-being and fulfillment.

At the heart of managing burnout is the recognition that it often signals a misalignment between one's values, actions, and environment. Burnout may arise when individuals find themselves pursuing goals that no longer resonate with their core values, working in environments that don't support their well-being, or neglecting their own needs in the pursuit of external validation or achievement. Understanding burnout as a symptom of deeper issues allows individuals to address it not merely as a temporary problem but as an opportunity for growth and transformation. This perspective enables people to view the journey not just as a process of recovery but as an opportunity to rebuild and realign their lives in a more meaningful and sustainable way.

The first step in this journey is to develop self-awareness, which involves understanding the signs and symptoms of burnout and recognizing its early indicators. Self-awareness enables individuals to identify when they are approaching burnout and to take action before it becomes severe. Regular check-ins with oneself—through mindfulness, journalism, or discussions with trusted friends or professionals—help maintain an understanding of personal stress levels, emotional state, and physical well-being. This awareness is the foundation upon which all other strategies are built, as it empowers individuals to respond proactively rather than creatively to the challenges they face.

Once self-awareness is established, the next step is to implement practical strategies for managing and preventing burnout. These strategies vary, from setting boundaries and developing healthy work-life integration to seeking support and building resilience. The process often involves trial and error as individuals explore different techniques and approaches to find what best supports their unique needs and lifestyle. Developing a personalized toolkit of strategies—such as mindfulness practices, exercise routines, social connections, and stress management techniques—provides individuals with the resources they need to navigate stressful periods without compromising their well-being.

An essential aspect of managing burnout is creating a supportive environment, both personally and professionally. On a personal level, this involves setting clear boundaries that protect time and energy, prioritizing self-care, and nurturing relationships that provide emotional support and connection. On a professional level, it may mean advocating for oneself in the workplace, communicating effectively with employers about workload and stress, and seeking or creating environments that value well-being and balance. The goal is to build a support system and environment that not only responds to burnout but actively works to prevent it.

Throughout this journey, it is important to recognize that managing burnout and finding balance is not a linear process. There will be ups and downs, and setbacks are a natural part of the journey. Individuals may experience periods of renewed energy and motivation, only to encounter new challenges that test their resilience. Accepting this non-linear path as part of the process is key to maintaining a long-term perspective. Building resilience and flexibility allows individuals to navigate these fluctuations with greater ease and to return to balance more quickly when they feel off course.

Your Road map to a Healthier, Happier Life

The journey of managing burnout and finding balance is deeply personal, but there are universal principles that can serve as a road map to guide individuals toward a healthier, happier life. This road map involves several interconnected elements: cultivating self-awareness, setting realistic goals, developing supportive habits, prioritizing self-care, and remaining open to growth and change.

1. Cultivating Self-Awareness: Self-awareness is the foundation of any meaningful change. It involves understanding your own patterns, recognizing your stress triggers, and being honest about your needs and limitations. Tools like mindfulness, journalism, and regular self-reflection help build this awareness, making it easier to identify when burnout is approaching and what adjustments are necessary. Building self-awareness also involves recognizing one's strengths and weaknesses, as well as understanding what environments and activities bring fulfillment and joy.

2. Setting Realistic Goals: Setting achievable, meaningful goals is crucial for maintaining balance. Often, burnout results from setting unrealistic expectations or striving to meet external pressures that conflict with one's own values and capabilities. By setting goals that align with personal values and breaking them into manageable steps, individuals create a sense of direction and progress without overwhelming themselves. Goal-setting should be flexible, allowing room for adjustment as circumstances change or as new priorities emerge. This flexibility ensures that goals remain a source of motivation rather than pressure, and it supports a sustainable approach to

growth and development.

3. Developing Supportive Habits: Sustainable, supportive habits are the building blocks of a balanced life. These habits include physical practices, such as regular exercise, sleep hygiene, and balanced nutrition, as well as mental and emotional practices, like meditation, gratitude journalism, or engaging in creative activities. Building habits that promote well-being requires consistency and commitment, but starting small and gradually integrating these habits into daily life makes them more sustainable. Over time, these habits become ingrained and provide the resilience needed to handle life's challenges without compromising well-being.

4. Prioritizing Self-Care: Self-care is not an indulgence; it is an essential component of managing burnout and maintaining balance. It involves carving out time for activities that replenish energy and nurture mental and emotional health. This can include anything from taking time for solitude and reflection to engaging in hobbies, spending time with loved ones, or simply resting. Prioritizing self-care also means learning to say no when necessary and setting boundaries that protect personal time and space. By treating self-care as a non-negotiable aspect of life, individuals ensure that their well-being remains a priority, preventing burnout and promoting long-term balance.

5. Remaining Open to Growth and Change: The journey of managing burnout and finding balance is dynamic, and it requires an openness to growth and adaptation. Life's circumstances and challenges are ever-changing, and maintaining balance involves staying flexible and willing to adjust as needed. This may mean revisiting and reassessing goals, exploring new opportunities for growth, or learning to adapt habits to fit different life stages. Openness to change also involves accepting that setbacks are part of the journey and viewing them as opportunities for growth rather than failures. A mindset that embraces change as a natural part of life enhances resilience and supports the long-term pursuit of balance.

For those committed to following this road map, the outcome is not simply the absence of burnout but the creation of a life that is both fulfilling and sustainable. A balanced life is one where individuals feel aligned with their values, energized by their work and personal activities, and supported by their relationships and environment. It is a life where challenges are met with resilience and where growth is seen as an opportunity for continuous improvement rather than a source of stress.

Ultimately, the process of managing burnout and finding balance is about reclaiming control over one's life. It is about making conscious choices that prioritize well-being, fulfillment, and growth over the pursuit of external validation or the compulsion to meet unrealistic standards. It is about building a life that supports not only short-term success but long-term happiness and health. The journey may be challenging, but with the right mindset, tools, and support, it is entirely possible to create a life where burnout is not an obstacle but a stepping stone toward a more balanced, purposeful, and joyful existence.

By embracing this road map and committing to the ongoing journey of self-discovery, growth, and balance, individuals can transform their experience of burnout into an opportunity for profound change and fulfillment. Each step taken—whether it's practicing mindfulness, setting boundaries, pursuing meaningful goals, or building resilience—contributes to a healthier, happier life where balance is not an endpoint but a continuous, evolving state that enhances overall well-being and quality of life.

www.ingramcontent.com/pod-product-compliance
Lightning Source LLC
Chambersburg PA
CBHW071050240526
45469CB00006BD/2283